D1458878

CHELSEA PAST

First published 1996
Reprinted 2001
by Historical Publications Ltd
32 Ellington Street, London N7 8PL
(Tel: 020-7607 1628)

ISBN 0 948667 39 7
British Library Cataloguing-in-Publication Data
A catalogue record for this book is available from the British Library

Typeset in Palatino by Historical Publications Ltd
Reproduction by G & J Graphics, London EC2
Printed by Edelvives in Zaragoza, Spain

CHELSEA PAST

Barbara Denny

HISTORICAL PUBLICATIONS

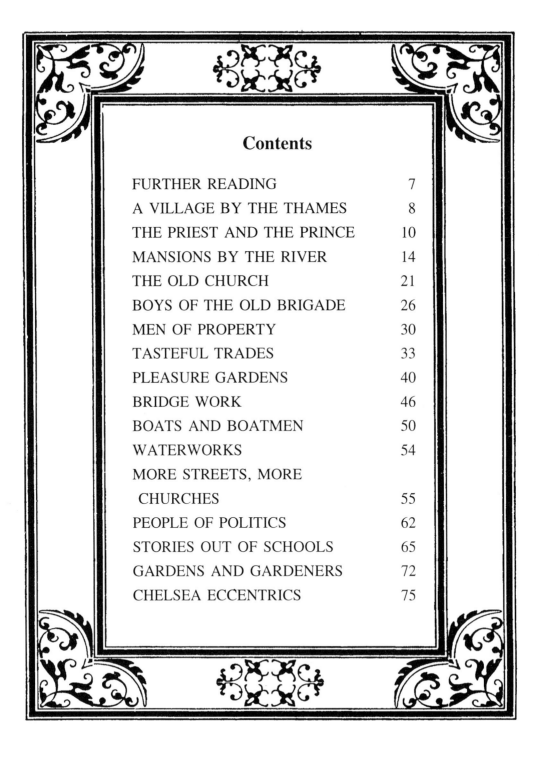

Contents

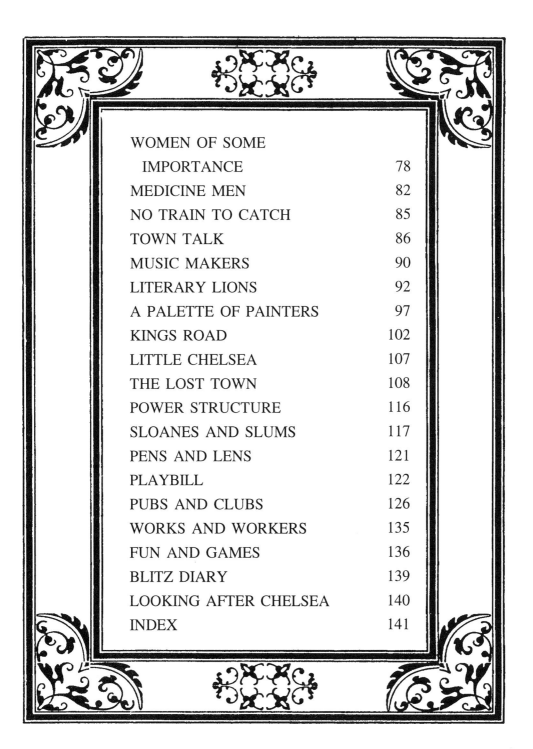

**To
Philip Denny**

Acknowledgements

In writing this book I have received very willing help from a number of people whom I have approached for information and assistance. These include Peter Osgood of Chelsea Yacht and Boat Co. Ltd; Michael Bryan for information and pictures from art exhibitions on Cheyne Walk and Old Chelsea; David Lowman of St Simon Zelotes; Christ Church; the Edith Grove Christian Centre; Mary Pascoe of Chelsea Methodists; Fr. Patrick Nolan of Our Most Holy Redeemer; Stephen Bury of Chelsea College of Art and Design; Melanie Gardner, Press and Information Officer, King's College; the Michael Parkin Gallery for exhibition material on Greaves and Whistler; Richard Dennison of Chelsea Pottery; the Octagon School; Hill House School; the Man in the Moon Theatre; Chelsea Theatre Centre; HAPA (Chelsea Adventure Playground); Tom Pocock of the Chelsea Society; and many others.

As usual I have had great help from Kensington & Chelsea Libraries' staff, especially from Carolyn Starren and Nicholas West of the Central and Chelsea Local Studies departments. I am indebted to the numerous authors of Chelsea that have gone before me: these are listed under Further Reading.

Lastly, but not least, I would like to thank my publisher and editor, John Richardson, for his disciplined but sensitive handling of my manuscript, and my husband, Philip Denny, who has to live with my books in embryo form for many months, but continues to encourage me.

The Illustrations

We are grateful to the following for permission to use illustrations as below:
Michael Bryan: *10, 17, 47, 52, 143, 162, 166, 169*
Chelsea College: *85, 86, 87*
Chelsea Football Club: *178*
Chelsea Harbour Estate Management: *148*
Chelsea Yacht and Boat Company: *61*
Roger Cline: *12, 14, 21, 41, 54, 93, 122, 133, 141*
Royal Borough of Kensington and Chelsea: *Jacket, 1, 22, 27, 39, 46, 48, 49, 51, 55, 56, 59, 60, 62, 65, 74, 78, 81, 90, 92, 102, 105, 106, 107, 108, 109, 110, 111, 124, 127, 134, 136, 137, 139, 142, 151, 154, 157, 159, 165, 167, 170, 172, 175, 178, 179*
Nesta Macdonald: *174*
National Portrait Gallery: *99*
Royal College of Music: *113*

All other illustrations were supplied by the Author and the Publisher. The illustrated maps were drawn by the Author.

Further Reading

Aldous, Tony: *London's Villages* (1980).
Barton, Nicholas: *The Lost Rivers of London* (1962; new edn 1992).
Beaver, Alfred: *Memorials of Old Chelsea* (1892).
Bignell, John: *Chelsea Seen from 1860 to 1980.*
Bloom, Ursula: *Rosemary for Chelsea* (1971).
Blunt, Reginald: *Paradise Row* (1906)
Blunt, Reginald: *In Cheyne Walk and Thereabout* (1914).
Blunt, Reginald: *The Wonderful Village* (1918).
Blunt, Reginald: *By Chelsea Reach* (1921).
Blunt, Reginald: *The Lure of Old Chelsea* (1922)
Borer, Mary Cathcart: *Two Villages: the story of Kensington and Chelsea* (1973).
Bowack, John: *Antiquities of Middlesex* (1705).
Bryan, Michael: *In Cheyne Walk and Thereabout* (1984).
Bryan, Michael: *Chelsea and the Thames* (1989).
Chelsea Society *Reports.*
Clark, Roger: *Chelsea Today* (1991).
Clunn, Harold P: *The Face of London* (1932; rev. 1972).
Curle, Brian: Leaflets on Shrewsbury House, and Kensington and Chelsea Libraries
Cuppleditch, David: *The London Sketch Club* (1979).
Davies, Randall: *The Greatest House at Chelsey* (1914)
Day, John R: *London's Underground* (1963).
Denny, Barbara and Starren, Carolyn: *Kensington and Chelsea in Old Photographs* (1995).
Denton, Penny (ed): *John Betjeman's London* (1988)
Duncan, Andrew: *Secret London* (1995).
Durrant, D.N: 'Shrewsbury House' in *History Today*, July 1974.
Ebel, S. and Wimpey, D: *London's Riverside* (1975).
Edmunds, Richard: *Chelsea Fields to Worlds End* (1956).
Faulkner, Thomas: *Historical and Topographical Description of Chelsea* (1829).
Froude, James Anthony: *Thomas Carlyle* (1891).
Gaunt, William: *Chelsea* (1958).
Gibson, Peter: *Capital Companion* (1985).
Holme, Thea: *Chelsea* (1972).
Howard, Philip: London's River (1975).
Logue, Christopher: *London in Verse* (1982).
Longford, Elizabeth, with Ditchburn, Jonathan: *Images of Chelsea* (1980).
Lysons, Daniel: *Environs of London* (1795).
Macdonald, Nesta: *The Pheasantry* (1977).
Massingham, Hugh and Pauline: *The London Anthology.*
Patterson, Alan: *Chelsea Physic Garden (1977).*
Pocock, Tom: *Chelsea Reach* (1970).
Silver, Harold and Teague, John: *Chelsea College – a History* (1978).
Survey of London volumes: *The Parish of Chelsea* (pt 1); *The Parish of Chelsea* (pt 2); *The Old Church; The Royal Hospital.*
Trench, Richard and Hillman, Ellis: *London Under London* (1985).
Turner, Christopher: *London Step by Step* (1994).
Walford, Edward: *Old and New London* Vol V (1892).
Walker, Annabel and Jackson, Peter: *Kensington and Chelsea: a social and architectural history* (1987).
Walkley, Giles: *Artists' Houses in London, 1764-1914* (1994).
Willson, G: *Nursery Gardens of West London* (1970).

A Village by the Thames

After London itself there can be few places in England more adjectival than Chelsea – its name is appended to Pensioners, a Flower Show, Porcelain, a Physic Garden, Arts, Buns, Old Church, Football Club, Harbour (though the latter two are in Fulham!). It is no wonder that it has retained its identity, despite being united with Kensington for municipal convenience. Chelsea has no natural sub-divisions, and it had only one town centre once the village had receded from that old highway, the Thames, to Kings Road. Today, the old Chelsea hamlet is a ghost around the old church, itself only a replica of the one practically destroyed during the last war, and a few precious remnants of houses along Cheyne Walk, glimpsed between the trees from the Embankment.

Yet this small part of London can claim more fame to the acre than almost any other, bristling with notable residents throughout six centuries, many of them important and crucial in the history of the country itself.

So how did it all begin?

Like much of London's history, with the river. As the City and Westminster became crowded with the mansions of the rich and the hovels of the poor, so London extended westwards along the Thames. In so doing, it enveloped the modest hamlet of Chelsea. The river features in the etymology of Chelsea as well, for the name is thought to derive from the Anglo Saxon *chesil*, meaning a gravel bank, though there are other suggestions such as *Cealchythe*, a landing place or wharf to unload barges carrying chalk.

A ford may have contributed to Chelsea's earliest habitation. The historian, William Maitland, wrote in 1730 of the discovery of a shallow passage in the river about 90 feet west of the present site of the Royal Hospital, which might have been where Julius Caesar crossed the Thames in 54BC.

In medieval times the manor of Chelsea consisted of a parish church, a manor house and a cluster of cottages; otherwise the terrain was of unreclaimed marshes, a low-lying frontage to the Thames which was frequently flooded, and wild woodland, which belonged to Westminster Abbey. Even in Victorian times the builder, Thomas Cubitt, had to transport excavated soil from his St Katharine's Docks enterprise to raise the levels of the new Belgravia above the tidal Thames.

Many residents of Chelsea made their living from fishing. John Stow in his *Survey of London* (1598) said that there was no river in Europe to compare with the Thames in its London reaches for 'fat, sweet salmon being taken daily from the stream'. (Henry VIII is said to have kept a polar bear at the Tower, which was let out on a leash to catch them.) There

1. *A view of Chelsea from the Thames, 1744, by Maurer.*

were also trout, roach, dace, flounders and eels.

There is a record of the parish church in Norman times, a building possibly preceded by a Saxon chapel. In 1290 it was named in papal letters as 'Chelchurche of All Saints', and from this it may be assumed that there was at that time enough 'chesil' bank, enough firm ground above tidal level, to allow building to take place.

The earliest recorded resident is Sir Reginald Bray, architect of the King Henry VII Chapel in Westminster Abbey and of St George's Chapel, Windsor, who was living at Chelsea Manor House in the early sixteenth century; the tomb of his nephew, Edmund, can still be seen in the Old Church. It was Bray's niece, Margaret, who married Sir William Sandys, friend of Thomas More, and inherited the manor at a time when Londoners were becoming dissatisfied with the overcrowded and insanitary conditions in the City. Throughout medieval times those who could afford to do so, and particularly ecclesiastical dignitaries, had built their mansions to the west of the City, mostly along the Strand, a trend confirmed in the sixteenth century when Thomas Wolsey, Archbishop of York, went even further, and built his magnificent palace in Whitehall, south of the village of Charing at the end of the Strand.

Wolsey was the patron of Thomas More, lawyer, theologian and philosopher. More chose to move even further westwards along the river and settled in Chelsea, then still in the country. He chose a plot about two hundred yards west of the Old Church to build a house which, according to his friend Desiderius Erasmus, was 'neither mean nor subject to envy, yet magnificent and commodious enough', a house quite in keeping with the view its owner had expounded in his *Utopia*, written a few years earlier, for 'a life of simple pleasure and modest comfort'.

After More, they all came, even the King himself, to set the royal accolade on what was known as the 'Village of Palaces'. Yet Chelsea was still a secluded, sparsely-populated rural area with only a few cottages between the new stately homes, in a parish of about 600 acres. Its boundaries were the stream on the west known variously as Counters Creek or Billingsditch, meandering down to the river through the marshy lands of Fulham; on the east there was another rivulet, the Westbourne, flowing from the hills of Hampstead, draining the marshes which were to become Pimlico and Belgravia and separating the parish of Chelsea from that of Westminster; to the north lay Kensington and Brompton beyond the road to Fulham. On the south, of course, was the Thames, both a boundary and a reason for existence. Across this lay the dismal marshes of Battersea, but behind them the fair prospect of the Surrey hills.

2. *A view of Chelsea and Chelsea Old Church in 1738.*

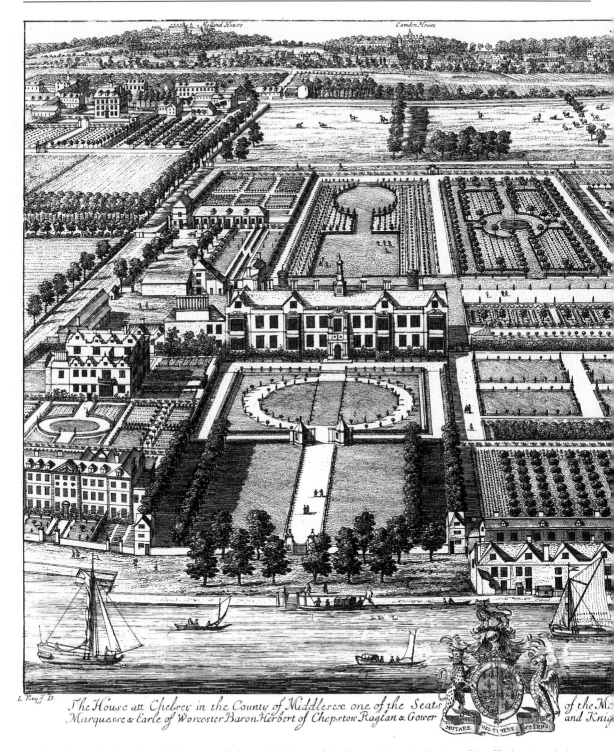

L. Kny f. D.

The House att Chelsey in the County of Middlesex one of the Seats
Marquesse & Earle of Worcester Baron. Herbert of Chepstow Raglan & Gower

MUTARE   VEL TIMERE   SPERNO

3. *'The House att Chelsey' in 1708 by L. Knyff, formerly the home of Sir Thomas More. At the time of Knyff's drawing, the house was called Beaufort House. On the horizon are Holland House, Campden House and what became Kensington Palace.*

Potent Prince Henry Duke of Beaufort
st Noble order of the Garter.

I. Kyp Sc

The Priest and the Prince

The story of Thomas More has been told so often that it can hardly bear retelling. But the story of Chelsea cannot be related without it. He was the first of its famous residents and his presence has never been erased – the survival of his chapel in the Old Church, after bombing, became a symbol of his endurance. More was a rebel, a man in advance of his time, of stubborn courage, who left his mark on English history.

His choice of Chelsea was due to the presence there of his old friend, Sir William Sandys. The site of his house is less definite. The Rev. Dr John King, Rector of Chelsea in the eighteenth century, and an enthusiastic historian, said: "As seven cities of Greece contended for the birthplace of Homer, there are no fewer houses in the parish which lay claim to be Sir Thomas More's residence." Later research, however, has settled firmly on a site roughly where Beaufort Street now runs south towards Battersea Bridge, and which was later to see the creation of Buckingham or Beaufort House, for More's mansion did not survive him in its original form for very long, being altered by successive owners over the next two centuries.

His nearest neighbour of repute would have been the Earl of Shrewsbury, who built a substantial house in about 1520, on a site which is now Oakley Street.

More was middle-aged when he moved out of the City of London where he was born and spent his youth. The son of a justice of the King's Bench, he was to follow his father in the legal profession; after schooldays at St Anthony's, Threadneedle Street, he was appointed as a page at Lambeth Palace in the household of the Archbishop of Canterbury, where the seeds of his future religious convictions were probably sown. These were furthered when he went up to Oxford, which was already astir with the controversies of the New Learning. Although he was to spend some years in legal study at the Inns of Court, the young More was already contemplating a religious life and in 1499 joined the Carthusian community of Charterhouse, London. A change of heart and mind is evident in the early years of the sixteenth century, when he was elected to Parliament and in his marriage the following year, 1505, to Jane Colt. It was a tragically short union as the unfortunate girl, having borne him four children, died in 1509. Seeking a mother for his orphaned brood, More settled on an intelligent City matron, the widowed Alice Middleton, who was to prove a stalwart consort in the troubled years ahead. This was also the year of the death of Henry VII, the first of the Tudor monarchs, and the succession of his son, Henry VIII.

4. Sir Thomas More, by Rubens.

Though More was already climbing the ladder of public appointments, he still found time for study and authorship – he wrote *Utopia*, an allegorical romance which presented More's imaginary humanist state, and which posed the problem of reconciling tolerant and liberal views with the dogmatism of the age. His views envisaged the marriage of priests, the higher education of women, cremation, euthanasia and the abolition of capital punishment.

And yet, in his later life while in power, his views became more intolerant, and in particular he pursued the Protestant, William Tyndale, translator of the Bible into English. As Lord Chancellor his duty was to 'search out heretics'.

More was appointed Under Treasurer to Henry VIII in 1520 at a time when Wolsey was all powerful among the King's advisers. It was about this time that More moved to Chelsea and there built a new house in red brick, with mullioned windows, around two courtyards with gate houses, chapel and library.

Despite a regular correspondence, Desiderius Erasmus does not seem to have been a visitor to Chelsea, but many others from the higher echelons of political and social life were members of a circle which revolved around the More residence. These included Bishop John Fisher of Rochester, John Stokesley, Bishop of London, John Heywood the poet and playwright, and Hans Holbein who illustrated *Utopia*, and who probably stayed with the family while he created the famous family portrait (see ill. 6), which has unfortunately only survived in its sketch

5. Hans Holbein, a self portrait.

form (now in the Basle Museum). The original huge painting, about 12 x 9 ft, is thought to have been lost in the fire at the Kremsier Palace in Moravia in 1792. However, before the painting disappeared, the More family did have copies made – one is at the National Portrait Gallery, and another was bought by the Chelsea Society in 1950 as a memorial to their founder, the historian Reginald Blunt. This is now hung at Chelsea Town Hall.

The portrait includes More and his wife, Lady Alice, his son John, and his daughter-in-law. Also there are his three daughters, their husbands and their children, as well as other relatives, retainers, and a jester, Henry Patterson. More was fond of animals and there are records of numerous dogs, an ape, a fox, ferrets, weasels and an aviary at Chelsea. Life seems to have been happy and affectionate, but strictly disciplined.

The most illustrious visitor was, of course, the King, who would sail up the river from London in his state barge, to talk with the man who after the disgrace of Wolsey, was to be his Lord Chancellor. As William Roper was later to record in his biography of his father-in-law, the two conferred on "matters of astronomy, geometry, divinity and worldly affairs". It was the latter which were eventually to lead to More's own downfall, as by 1530 Henry was moving towards his 'great matter' – the divorce from his wife, Catherine of Aragon, who in twenty years had borne him only one live child, Mary Tudor, and a new marriage to Anne Boleyn. The 'great matter' had already contributed to the fall of Wolsey, and when the King went his own way and divorced Catherine, More resigned the Chancellorship. While More retired to Chelsea, Thomas Cranmer, his successor as Lord Chancellor, pursued the Protestant revolution and the dissolution of the monasteries, policies which led to the break from Rome and the establishment of the Church of England.

Henry's declaration that he was supreme head of the Church in England was opposed by More. Knowing that his action would be deemed treasonable, More left Chelsea on 17 April 1534 and after making his confession to Dr Lark, the Rector of Chelsea, took a boat to Lambeth where he made a formal refusal of the Supremacy Oath. He was detained in the Tower for fifteen months under sentence of death, and despite opportunities to es-cape punishment, he accepted his execution. His daughter Margaret rescued his severed head, which had been placed on a pole on London Bridge, and secured its interment in her husband's family vault at St Dunstan's, Canterbury. The body was interred, as was the custom with Tower prisoners, in the chapel there of St Peter ad Vincula, though whether it remained there is not known. John Aubrey, in his *Brief Lives*, thought that it had been removed to Chelsea church. Another theory suggests that it was then transferred, with the later removal of coffins, to the new parish church of St Luke's in the 1870s.

In 1886 More was beatified by the Roman Catholic Church and in 1935 canonised.

The chapel and black marble tablet in the old Chelsea church had been commissioned by More himself in 1528, while he was still in royal favour. This, anticipating his own demise, commemorates not only his first wife Jane, but also himself and Lady Alice. "Ah, how well could we three have lived together did faith and religion permit, but the tomb shall unite us I pray and death give us what life could not."

6. *Sir Thomas More, his family and servants. A sketch of a now lost painting, though a copy exists in the National Portrait Gallery.*

Mansions by the river

A ROYAL RESIDENCE

Whatever Henry's regrets or memories of his erstwhile servant, Thomas More, they did not deter him from owning land in Chelsea. Within months of his former friend's death he had acquired the manor from Lord Sandys in exchange for an estate in Hampshire and was busy with plans for his own large riverside mansion. The site for this new house was to the east of the present Oakley Street, in the vicinity of nos. 19-26 Cheyne Walk. Faulkner's *History of Chelsea* contains a print which shows it as a long, two-storey building with high chimney stacks and a partly-castellated roof line. It was certainly spacious, with over thirty rooms as well as banqueting halls and three kitchens. In the years ahead it was to become a sort of dower house and nursery for Henry's discarded wives and their children. Indeed, by the time the new mansion was completed, Henry's marriage with Anne Boleyn was over, she had met her death on Tower Hill in 1536, and the King's third wife, Jane Seymour, had died in 1537 giving birth to a sickly boy, who would become Edward VI. Edward and his half-sister, Anne's daughter Elizabeth, were installed at Chelsea under the guardianship of a lady of the Court.

The last of Henry's wives, Catherine Parr, was given the manor of Chelsea as part of her marriage portion, and lived there as a widow with the step-children, with visits from the luckless Jane Grey, a studious girl of eleven. Other frequent visitors were the Duke of Somerset, uncle of the boy king Edward and Lord Protector during his minority, and the Duke's brother, Thomas Seymour, Lord High Admiral.

Thomas Seymour, ambitious for higher office, saw a path to it through a judicious marriage. His choice of the widowed queen may have been obvious, but the young Elizabeth was more attractive and soon tongues were wagging about his flirtatious behaviour with her. Seymour eventually lost his head, but for other misdemeanours. The Lord Protector Somerset also soon fell from grace and was executed in 1552. His successor, John Dudley, Duke of Northumberland met a similar fate, for his plan to place his niece, Jane Grey, on the throne after the death of Edward VI. Surprisingly, the widows of both Somerset and Northumberland were permitted to live at Chelsea after their husbands had lost their heads. Also resident in this extraordinary household was Henry's most fortunate, though plainest wife, Anne of Cleves, who spent her last years here before her death in 1557.

She was the last royal occupant of Chelsea's Tudor mansion, though Queen Elizabeth used to make frequent visits to see her old friend, Lord Howard

7. The north front of Henry VIII's mansion, as depicted in Thomas Faulkner's History of Chelsea.

of Effingham, who was granted the house as a grace and favour residence.

Elizabeth had another reason to visit Chelsea, for by 1596 Thomas More's old house was occupied by her Secretary of State, Sir Robert Cecil, who had inherited it from his father, Lord Burleigh. This house, after More's death, had been handed over to Sir William Pawlett, a wily statesmen who survived the turbulent times. Eventually the house passed to his son's step-daughter, Lady Dacre and her husband, and it was she who bequeathed it to Lord Burleigh. By 1627 the house was called Buckingham House (after its then resident, the 1st Duke of Buckingham). Seized by the government during the Commonwealth period, it was later sold to Henry, Marquess of Worcester (later the Duke of Beaufort) who gave it its last name, Beaufort House, and spent a great deal of money on improvements which the diarist, John Evelyn, considered 'ill-contrived and a waste of money.'

The Beauforts moved on and in 1736, when the house had stood empty for some years, it was bought by Sir Hans Sloane for £2,500, and demolished about three years later for the development of the whole surrounding area. All that was saved was the Inigo Jones gate, which Sloane presented to Lord Burlington and which is still at Chiswick House.

CHELSEA MANOR HOUSE

The original modest Chelsea Manor House, which the Sandys family had been occupying when Henry VIII acquired the manor, was taken in the later years of the sixteenth century by Sir Thomas Lawrence, a London goldsmith – his name is commemorated in Lawrence Street, and his death in 1593 is recorded in the family chapel in the Old Church. The chapel, however, is a fourteenth-century building and it is likely that Lawrence acquired it together with the manor, and the chapel was renamed after him. The family did, however, remain in Chelsea for another hundred years or more, as a great grandson of Sir Thomas, bearing the same name, sold the manor house, possibly by then rebuilt, to the Duchess of Monmouth in 1712. The Dowager Duchess had married James Scott, the 'Protestant Duke' and illegitimate son of Charles II, when he was only 14 years old. He was executed after the Monmouth Rebellion of 1685.

In 1749, when the old manor house had been divided into two or three dwellings, one of the residents was the writer, Tobias Smollett (see p92). In its final days the building was used as part of the Chelsea porcelain factory and was demolished in 1830.

8. The Lawrence family monument in Old Church.

GORGES HOUSE

In 1600 the eccentric Earl of Lincoln was in brief occupation of More's old home and to the east of it, he built another house for his daughter and her husband, Sir Arthur Gorges. Gorges House later became a girls' boarding school run by Josiah Priest, and is still described as a school for young ladies by Bowack in 1705. Very shortly after this it must have been sold to the Milman family, for soon it was demolished to make way for a group of cottages, Milmans Row. These in turn deteriorated in Victorian times and were themselves replaced by the borough council's Cremorne Estate in 1952.

9. Gorges House in 1705; drawn by Alfred Beaver, 1890.

THE FIRST GARDENER

Chelsea's long association with horticulture cannot have had a better beginning that the arrival early in the seventeenth century of Sir John Danvers (1588-1655), whose house was built on land much of which is now occupied by Paultons Square. Sir John was described as of such great personal beauty that people would follow him in the street, even if his political loyalties during the Civil War were dubious. He was an enthusiastic gardener and a tolerant husband, taking a liberal view of his wife's devotion to poet-priest John Donne. According to John Aubrey in *Brief Lives*, Danvers was the first "to teach the way of Italian gardens". These broke from the formal, rather dull fashion of the Tudor period in favour of romantic bowers and arbours, interspersed with fountains and statues. Aubrey described the garden to the north of the house as being planted with lilacs, sweet briars and fruit trees, and to the south, opening on to vistas towards the Thames and Surrey.

The core of Danvers House had been known as 'the More House', and was either the place to which More's widow retired, or the home of his daughter Margaret and her husband, William Roper.

In 1625 Danvers married, rather surprisingly, a widow at least twenty years older than himself, Magdalen Herbert, mother of the poet and hymn-writer, George Herbert. He is said to have "loved her for her wit" and so apparently did the widower, John Donne, nearer to her age than her husband, who came to stay with them in Chelsea, his own wife having died in 1617 at the age of 33 after giving birth to their twelfth child. Only two years after his arrival, Magdalen died and Donne wept as he preached at her funeral in the Old Church, quoting the famous lines "No Spring, no Summer beauty hath such grace as I have seen in one autumnal face."

Danvers soon recovered from his bereavement, marrying the following year Elizabeth Dauntsey, the heiress of a Wiltshire estate where he could indulge his taste for gardening on an even larger scale. After her death he married for the third time in 1648, and it was in that year he was a participant in the trial of Charles I and was a co-signatory to his death warrant. His own death in 1655 saved him from certain prosecution as a regicide at the Restoration.

Danvers' house was later taken by Lord John Robartes, who became Lord Radnor, and whose beautiful young wife, Laetitia Isabella, set London talking with her flirtatious ways. Her old husband was described as "sour and cynical" and after a while, following her association with the King's brother, James, Duke of York, packed her off to the country on a pilgrimage to "end her barrenness". It

10. Sir John Danvers is commemorated in Danvers Street, which is built across the grounds of his old house. This view entitled 'Duke Street from Lombard Street' was painted by Henry and Walter Greaves.

11. Gough House, from a drawing by J. Rush. This mansion, between the Physic Garden and the grounds of the Royal Hospital, was built by John Vaughan, 3rd Earl of Carbery, at the end of the 17th century. It escaped destruction when the Embankment was built and was used to house the Victoria Hospital for Children.

apparently worked for on her return she bore him six children to add to the five he already had from his first marriage, one of whom, a daughter, was christened 'Essex' to commemorate the Earl under whom he fought at the battle of Edgehill. Laetitia survived her husband, who died in 1685, to become the second wife of Charles Cheyne.

The last occupant of Danvers House in the last years of the seventeenth century was Thomas (later Marquis of) Wharton, a leading Whig politician described by Jonathan Swift as "a protestant in politics and an atheist in religion', and who is said to have written the words of *Lilli Burlero* to the music of Purcell, a song which became associated with the drive to oust James II. Wharton was the landowner of the extensive area which became known as Chelsea Park and which shortly after his departure was used for a venture in the cultivation of mulberries for silk manufacture (see p36).

In 1716 came the end of Danvers House and by 1729 houses in Danvers Street were being advertised. At the beginning of the nineteenth century, before the building of Paultons Square, Shepherds Nursery occupied what had long before been Sir John Danvers' lovely garden.

THE OTHER QUEEN BESS

The last of the early Chelsea mansions near the riverside was Shrewsbury House. Even today its ghost remains, seen occasionally in a fragment of a wall, or in the garden of a new town house – two houses in Oakley Street have gardens which were once part of its estate – and in the lines of old maps and plans. Today, a block of flats of the same name stands on the site which was only identified a few years ago by the discovery of an early plan of the house.

Shrewsbury House was erected by the Earl of Shrewsbury in 1520, at almost the same time as Thomas More and others were being attracted to Chelsea, and just after the birth of one of its most remarkable future inhabitants, the notorious Elizabeth ('Bess') Hardwick, of Hardwick Hall in Derbyshire, who was destined to marry the Earl's grandson. Bess Hardwick's fourth husband, in 1568, was the 6th Earl of Shrewsbury, who bitterly regretted the match, discovering too late that she had "a greedy appetite for money". When he died in 1590 her marriage portion was returned to her, which, plus the estates of her previous husbands, added to the family seat of Hardwick Hall, made her the wealthi-

12. *Shrewsbury House, the home of the formidable Bess Hardwick 1591-2.*

est woman in England next to Queen Elizabeth. When she came to London on the death of her last husband she had the choice of four Shrewsbury houses to stay at, but her preference was the Chelsea residence, which was maintained by a small staff under a steward. The arrival of the Countess and her retinue of forty people, family and servants, must have produced pandemonium in Chelsea.

She arrived on 24 November 1591 and stayed until the following July, when she returned with the same pomp and ceremony to Hardwick Hall, where she remained another sixteen years, quarrelling with everyone.

In its heyday, Shrewsbury House had two wings of uneven length, built on to a central building, with a huge garden that to the east spread across what is now Oakley Street. But by 1813, when it was named Alston House after Joseph Alston, who had bought it in *c*.1660, it was derelict. It was broken up and sold piecemeal, and replaced by shops and wharves; in the 1930s there was further development, including a handsome house by Edwin Lutyens, which had an amazingly short life.

Shrewsbury/Alston House had a new neighbour when the Duke of Hamilton built a large residence to the east of Oakley Street which shortly afterwards became the London palace of the bishops of Winches-

ter. It is described as "a heavy brick building of low proportions and quite devoid of any architectural ornament, the interior fairly commodious and much enriched by collections of antiques placed there by its last occupant Bishop Brownlow North." Earlier residents had included the notorious Benjamin Hoadley, who as Bishop of Bangor preached a doctrine of Christianity "without creed, order or discipline", a philosophy which shocked high churchmen and led to such a stormy dispute in Convocation that the assembly was prorogued for many years. Hoadley died at Chelsea in 1761, and the house survived until 1828.

CHELSEA COLLEGE

The Winchester palace was not the only ecclesiastical establishment in Chelsea. James I had given his blessing to a scheme instituted by the Rev. Dr Mathew Sutcliffe, Dean of Exeter, to set up a college at Chelsea to study 'polemic divinity' (theological controversy). The site chosen was on the eastern boundary of the parish near the Five Fields and the outlet of the Westbourne, leased from the Lord of Chelsea manor, the High Admiral Lord Howard of Effingham (created the Earl of Nottingham in 1597). To this land the King donated another 22 acres of adjacent Crown

13. *Winchester Palace, London home of the Bishops of Winchester.*

14. *The projected extent of the Theological College, Chelsea, though it is doubtful if much of it became a reality.*

property and Dr Sutcliffe himself promised to contribute generously to the building costs. The King, who laid the foundation stone in 1609, gave timber from the oaks in Windsor Park.

There were to be, apart from the Provost (Sutcliffe), seventeen clerical Fellows and two lay historians. The large building proposed was around a double quadrangle and was flanked by towers and side wings. Very little of it was ever built. Although the list of appointments was imposing, including a number of bishops and theological scholars, very few Fellows took up their posts – there was not the money for stipends. Furthermore, its establishment provoked hostility on all sides. William Laud, Archbishop of Canterbury called it 'Controversy College' before he himself became controversial enough to lose his head.

Sutcliffe impoverished himself in attempting to support the College. On his death, his successor was Dr Featley, a Calvinist who managed to quarrel with the puritans and was imprisoned. A later Provost was the royalist Rector of Chelsea, Dr Samuel Wilkinson, described by Parliamentarians as "a man of very scandalous report".

In 1651 the Commonwealth administration enquired whether the then almost derelict college could be utilised for housing Scots prisoners. After the Restoration the building was used again as a prison, this time for men taken in the Dutch wars. John Evelyn, one of the Commissioners appointed to the charge of these unfortunates, was very concerned about their conditions at Chelsea, reporting to Samuel Pepys that the wounded were dying like dogs, that others were smitten with plague and the rest were starving.

In June 1664 the recently established Royal Society sought to take over the building, a request granted by the King, although by then the place was in a ruinous state. By 1678 the tiles were taken off and the timber was stored to prevent further decay. Plans to convert it to a market garden, an observatory, or an extension to a glass-blowing laboratory came to nothing.

In the end, its site was taken by the Royal Military Hospital, which in its early years was also known, confusingly, as a 'College'.

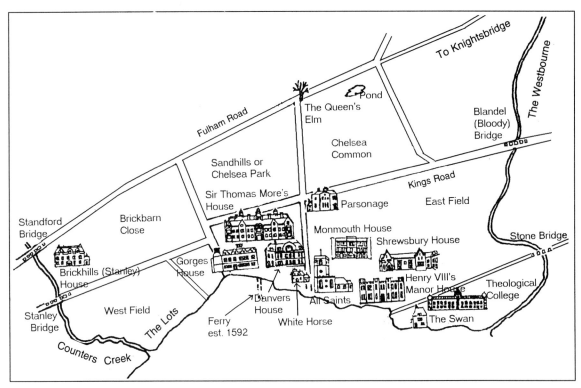

15. *Principal buildings in Chelsea 1520-1630. Brickhills (Stanley) House c1637, rbt c1690; Sir Thomas More's House c1520, rebt (as Buckingham) 1600, then Beaufort, dem. 1740; Gorges House 1567, rbt 1590, dem. c.1720; Henry VIII's mansion 1536, dem c.1750-5; Shrewsbury House c1540, dem. 1813; All Saints c.1300; Theological College 1618-80; Parsonage House c.1566; Monmouth (Lawrence) House c.1500-1835; The Swan c.1600-1780; White Horse c.1550, rebt 1840; Danvers House c.1620-1716.*

16. South-east view of the Old Church in 1750, by Chatelaine.

The Old Church

Sentiment has a lot to do with fashion. In the 1870s, Edward Walford, the Victorian historian and co-author of the series of volumes entitled *Old and New London*, considered Chelsea Old Church "by no means conspicuous for beauty.... sadly incongruous and much barbarised", although conceding that the interior was "still picturesque". By the time Alfred Beaver wrote his *Memorials of Old Chelsea* in 1892, this view had mellowed somewhat as he described it as "plain and unpretentious but having a beauty in humility". Much of the criticism of the church was due to it having been "erected piecemeal at different periods", which was true.

The first record of a church at *Chelcheth* – All Saints – is found in a Papal taxation document in 1291 and the first Rector is mentioned in a will of 1314. The title 'Old Church' is comparatively modern, dating from the building of the new parish church of St Luke in Sydney Street in 1821, when All Saints (sometimes also confusingly known as St Luke's) became too small for the growing population.

An inventory of church possessions in the reign of Edward VI lists plate, ornaments, jewels, chalices and crosses at All Saints, the gift of Thomas More, many of which had already been sold and which

More had predicted would "soon be taken away by bad men". The remaining treasures were later put into a collection of church plate for display at the Victoria & Albert Museum, where they remain today.

Manorial records of 1667 describe the church by the river as being "much decayed" and too small to contain its congregation, "divers great and noble personages" having moved into the district resulting in the situation whereby "many ancient inhabitants and families were finding themselves too often excluded from worship."

Bowack, writing in 1705, tells how "the shattered tower and west end were pulled down and the north and south aisles carried several yards to the west, windows enlarged, old parts beautified and new pews installed." The churchyard was raised and enclosed by a brick wall, all this being carried out between 1667 and 1674. The cost was met by donations from the parishioners, including Lady Jane Cheyne: she paid for the construction of the new roof. To carry out these works a new wharf was constructed to unload materials from the Thames.

The new brick tower, 113ft to the vane on the top of the cupola, and originally battlemented, was the highest brick-built edifice in the country, but shook

17. Looking west from Prospect Place to the Old Church and Arch House; painting by Walter Greaves.

when the bells rang. It had to be repaired and rebraced several times. During the building of St Luke's in 1821, the safety of the Old Church tower was again in question, and it was decided to remove the bells, smelt them down, and use the proceeds towards the peal at the new church.

A hundred and twenty years later the Old Church was to become a phoenix-like symbol of faith and resurrection. On the night of 16 April 1941, during one of the worst raids on London, the building was reduced to a shell, its tower shattered and its interior a mass of broken masonry and protruding timbers. In daylight it was found that despite the terrible damage, the More and Lawrence Chapels were practically intact, and prompt action by the incumbent, Ralph Sadleir, the architect and antiquary Walter Godfrey, and the Borough Engineer ensured that sensitive salvage work was carried out.

Restoration work, directed by Godfrey, began in 1950 and in July that year the More Chapel was opened for services, followed shortly by the Lawrence Chapel. In 1958, the church was rededicated and consecrated by the Bishop of London in the presence of Queen Elizabeth the Queen Mother, who was also present in July 1964 when the refurbished

More chapel was rededicated as a Lady Chapel.

The memorials which survived the bombing include the magnificent monument to Lord and Lady Dacre, who lived in More's old home in the 1590s. Lady Anne lies in marble Elizabethan finery beside her bearded husband in soldier's armour. In the south-east corner of the church is the tomb of Jane Guildford, Duchess of Northumberland, who died in 1555 only a year after the execution of her husband for plotting to put Jane Grey on the throne (see p14). Despite this, however, she is said to have had the most magnificent funeral ever seen at the church.

The oldest monument is undoubtedly that of the Bray family, although its inscriptions are worn away. There are records of the burial of Edmund, the first Lord Bray, the early Tudor lord of the manor, and other members of his family. His son, John Bray, was interred after a funeral procession by barge from Blackfriars in November 1557.

The pious Lady Jane Cheyne is commemorated by a life-size recumbent figure in white Carrara marble, the work of the sculptor Antonio Raggi, who was told by her mourning husband in 1699 to "make her in her habit as she lived".

Later memorials include those to William de Morgan

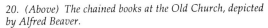

18. *(Left) The Stanley Monument in Old Church; drawn by Alfred Beaver (1890).*

19. *(Below) The Old Church by W. Alister Macdonald (1908), after the formation of the Embankment. Compare with illustration 17.*

20. *(Above) The chained books at the Old Church, depicted by Alfred Beaver.*

21. *Looking down Old Church Street towards the Old Church and the river; photograph by James Hedderley.*

22. *Chelsea Rectory in pre-war days*

(*d*.1917), Henry James (*d*.1916), and a tribute to the famous women academics of Chelsea, erected by the Federation of University Women which at one time occupied Crosby Hall on the Embankment.

Also in the church are a seventeenth-century altar and font base and, most remarkably of all, the antique books which Hans Sloane gave to the church – these are the only surviving chained books in London. They include a 'Vinegar' Bible (in which the word 'vineyard' is spelt 'vinegar', and an original copy of Foxe's *Book of Martyrs*. Also saved from the bombing was the Ashburnham Bell, given to the church in 1679 by the Hon. William Ashburnham as a thanksgiving for being saved from the river on a foggy night by hearing the striking of the church bell, which guided his boatman to safety.

THE RECTORY

A Rectory was first noted in Chelsea in 1327, though its site is unknown, and in Elizabethan days a 'Parsonage House' is said to have been next to More's house (approximately Milmans Street). In 1766 the Rector was permitted to let off parts of the church lands for building purposes, provided that the Rectory House and its gardens remained intact: thus the kitchen garden became Glebe Place and part of Bramerton Street and Kings Road.

Dr John King, Rector from 1694 to 1732, produced a history of the parish in manuscript which has supplied later historians with some valuable records of his time. He inherited the Rectory building in such a poor state that he had to take lodgings in Old Church Street.

Subsequent rectors included the Rev. William Cadogan, who invited John Wesley into the pulpit, Dr Gerald Wellesley, brother of the Duke of Wellington, and the Rev. Charles Kingsley, father of the two author brothers, Charles and Henry. Charles is best known for his allegorical fairy tale, *The Water Babies*, rather than for his historical novels, and Henry, whose *The Hilliers and the Burtons*, a fascinating account of nineteenth-century Chelsea, is almost forgotten. The Rev. Gerald Blunt, appointed in 1860, was the father of the Chelsea historian and founder of the Chelsea Society, Reginald Blunt.

The Rectory garden was also the setting for the first Adventure Playground for physically handicapped children. With the sale of the Rectory, the playground moved to a corner of the grounds of the Royal Hospital. This continues today, with play organised for children with and without disabilities by full-time staff and volunteers.

The Rectory and its huge garden, one of the largest private gardens in London, was the subject of long redevelopment speculations but was eventually sold into private use in the 1980s.

Boys of the Old Brigade

Although tales of the association of Nell Gwynne with the founding of the Chelsea Royal Hospital are dismissed as fanciful by historians, the true story has great interest, if not romance. The main characters are Charles II, his Paymaster General, Stephen Fox, Christopher Wren and the civil servant, John Evelyn, who had been one of the Commissioners for the Sick, Wounded and Prisoners of the Dutch Wars, and whose detailed diaries have left us a vivid picture of the age.

Charles II was very conscious of his debt to the army, having already made a pledge to his loyal troops at Tangier that whatever befell them they would always be in his care, and he had been impressed by the Hôtel des Invalides in Paris, provided by Louis XIV for his own old soldiers. When Fox suggested a similar institution in England, Charles was enthusiastic.

It was a difficult time for any Paymaster General. The country had had to withstand the ravages and expense of the Great Plague, the Great Fire and the Dutch Wars and even serving soldiers were paid infrequently. So, the problem of finding the money for a soldiers' hospital was not an easy one to solve.

The site was not difficult to procure – the 'Controversial College' at Chelsea described on pp.18-20, had been taken over by the Royal Society, but they didn't know what to do with it. The land was therefore bought back for the Crown for £13,000 and building work commenced with the financial support of the King and Fox (though not the Archbishop of Canterbury, who declined to help), and the architectural skills of Christopher Wren, then in the middle of supervising the rebuilding of London.

The foundation stone was laid by the King in 1682 and by the time of his death work was well forward. Wren had been commissioned to produce accommodation for the "relief and reception of four companies [about four hundred men] as in a college or monastery". A library was included.

James II continued to encourage the scheme, this time in association with Stephen Fox's son, Charles, who had succeeded his father as Paymaster General. But the two men fell out and the post was given instead to Richard Jones, the 1st Earl Ranelagh, an unscrupulous rogue who was more interested in building his own mansion in the Hospital grounds. He was later charged with fraud and dismissed.

The Hospital was completed in 1692 and despite later additions by Robert Adam and John Soane, has

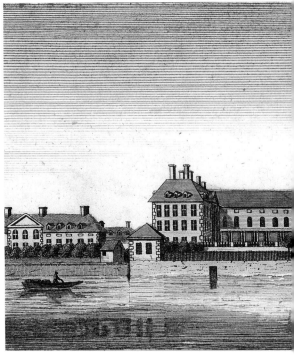

23. *The south front of Chelsea Hospital, c.1750*

changed very little since, with its great central quadrangle (Figure Court), and the Doric portico and colonnade before the entrance to the Great Hall and Chapel, on which a Latin inscription pays tribute to its royal patrons. In the centre of the quadrangle is a bronze statue of Charles in Roman warrior's garb by Grinling Gibbons, which was presented by Tobias Rustat, the Page of the Back Staircase, whom Evelyn described as a "very simple, ignorant but honest creature." It is round this statue that the old soldiers parade on Founder's Day on 29 May each year, a date which commemorates the escape by the future Charles II from the Parliamentary forces at the battle of Worcester. This ceremony, when the salute is taken by a member of the Royal Family, is one of the most moving in London's public calendar, as the elderly men march, remarkably erect despite their age and disabilities, to the music of a regimental band playing *The Boys of the Old Brigade*.

To the east and west of the quadrangle are the Light Horse and College Courts, the former being the location of the Governor's quarters, including the splendid Board Room with its art collection. The Chapel, with its black and white marble floor, carvings by Gibbons and Sebastian Ricci frescoes, was consecrated in August 1691 and over the centuries has housed the captured standards of bygone wars.

24. Pensioners outside the porticoed entrance in the 1920s.

The Great Hall was intended to resemble a college refectory, but it also served many large occasions such as the lying-in-state of the Duke of Wellington in 1852, concerts, military courts etc. It also houses some of the Hospital's works of art, including a large equestrian painting of Charles II by Antonio Verrio.

The pensioners, housed in the east and west sides of Figure Court and in the new buildings reconstructed in replica after war damage, are selected from a huge number of eligible applicants who must be on permanent pensions, have no dependants and have "given good service by flood and field". They occupy cubicles which give cosy privacy.

Traditionally, their diet consisted of beef on Sundays and mutton on weekdays (until a petition asked for bacon once a week), and a pint of porter and a pennyworth of tobacco every day. Modernisation has brought a more varied diet, and also the installation of many more bathrooms, lifts, central heating, radios and reading lamps.

The pensioners' uniform has remained almost unchanged – scarlet coats in the summer and navy blue in the winter, with the peaked shako (tricorns on dress occasions). The administration structure is virtually the same as at foundation – a Governor, a Lieutenant Governor, Adjutant, Medical Officer, Chaplain and Quartermaster, and six Captains of

Invalids who are responsible for the day-to-day maintenance and order. Although it was felt that Army discipline might be unwelcome in old age, it is enjoyed by men who have spent long years in service and certainly the longevity of many of the inmates indicates a tranquillity of mind.

Originally, the burial ground for pensioners, designed by Wren, was in the grounds of the Hospital, and here lie such old soldiers as Robert Comming who died in 1767 at the reputed age of 116, among 10,000 others who spent there last days here over a period of more than 200 years. This graveyard also commemorates two women 'out pensioners', who asked to be laid there. They are Hannah Snell (d.1792) and Christiana Davis (d.1739), who served in the Army in disguise. In 1854 burials here ceased and a special plot was allocated to pensioners at Brompton Cemetery, but nowadays interments take place at Brookwood in Surrey.

The extensive grounds of the Hospital were landscaped by Wren and, in those days, ran right down to the river, with two forty-foot canals on either side. The obelisk which is now the centre point of the marquee at the Chelsea Flower Show was erected in 1853 in memory of officers and men of the 24th Regiment who died at Chillinawalla in the Sikh War in 1849.

25. *Pensioners dining in the Great Hall, as depicted by Pugin and Rowlandson c.1808.*

Until late Victorian days the pensioners cultivated plots of land in the Hospital grounds and on Sundays the little gardens, over 140 in number, were open to the public, who could buy posies from the old men. In 1687 a piece of land to the north of the Hospital had been bought from Lord Cheyne with the intention of providing a grand drive to the frontage from Kings Road but this was never carried out, the ground being used as a hayfield and eventually becoming Burtons Court open space and cricket pitch.

Nowadays the grounds and courtyards of the Hospital are open to the public every day, and various parts of the buildings are accessible at more specific times. There is a museum of military memorabilia, and nearby is the National Army Museum with a more extensive display of British military history, which includes Wellington's shaving mirror and Florence Nightingale's lamp.

26. *Pensioners in the grounds of the Hospital in the 1920s.*

27. *A late-Victorian pensioner and his pet.*

Men of Property

THE FIRST CHEYNE

All the great property-owning families of London have left an indelible mark upon the districts they owned – the Bedfords, Grosvenors, Portlands, Cavendishes, Gunters and so many others, but none more so than the Sloanes and Cadogans. Not only is there a legacy of street names, but the character and appearance of their developed Chelsea estates are very much of their doing.

The story might have been different if the beautiful Jane Cavendish, daughter of the Duke of Newcastle, had not fallen in love with Charles Cheyne, a Buckinghamshire squire, in the mid seventeenth century. 'Fallen in love' is perhaps a romanticism, for she was not a girl, being over thirty when she chose him "for his virtue" and politics as much as for his physical attractions. The courageous Lady Jane and her sister, Elizabeth, had defended one of their father's homes against Parliamentary forces while he was in exile, and she had resolved to marry "no-one who had ill-treated her king and her father", although there were few left of these in England, at least of her social class, in the 1650s.

The ancient Cavendish family split at about this time to produce in one branch the Dukes of Newcastle and in the other, the Dukes of Devonshire. Jane, though, was not an heiress, but when she married Charles Cheyne in 1655 she brought enough of a dowry with her for him to buy the 'New Manor House' – the mansion built by Henry VIII and in which the King installed his discarded wives and children (see p.14). An inventory of Jane's jewels lists a necklace of pearls valued at £725 (the annual salary of a high court official), and a pair of lockets "wherein are 18 great diamonds and 16 little ones worth £342". The 'New Manor' had been sequestered after the conviction and execution of its earlier occupant, the Royalist Duke of Hamilton, but sold back after the Restoration to his trustees. The Cheynes had probably already settled in Chelsea where Jane had relations, probably at Blacklands House on Chelsea Common, nearer to Knightsbridge. They renamed the new home Chelsea Place and carried out many improvements to the house and garden, which were much admired by the diarist John Evelyn.

The marriage was short lived, Jane dying at the age of 49 in 1669, long before her husband was created Viscount Newhaven in 1681. They had three children, the eldest son, William Cheyne, inheriting the property on his father's death in 1698.

28. *Sir Hans Sloane, from the painting by Stephen Slaughter, 1736.*

29. *Sloane's monument in All Saints' churchyard.*

SIR HANS SLOANE

William Cheyne did not share his father's affection for Chelsea, and valued his land holdings there for their financial potential rather than anything else. Very soon, building sites were being marked out for Cheyne Row and the first houses in Cheyne Walk. In 1712 the manor was sold to Sir Hans Sloane, famous physician, antiquary and collector.

As a medical student Sloane had often visited the Apothecaries' garden at Chelsea. His brilliance as a scholar is evident from his election to the Royal

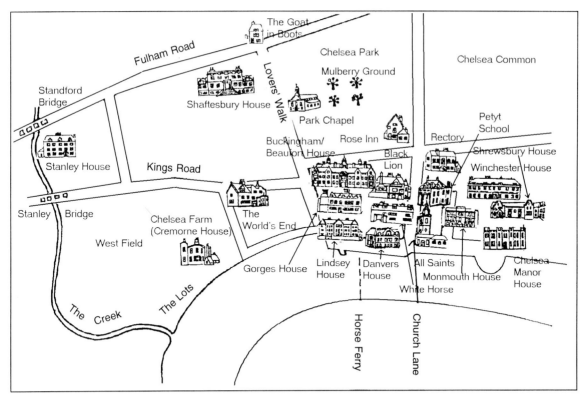

30. The principal buildings of West Chelsea 1630-1750. All Saints rebuilt c.1667; Black Lion c.1690; Buckingham/Beaufort House (formerly More's house) rebuilt 1680, dem. 1740; Chelsea Farm c.1740 (Cremorne House), dem. 1877; Danvers House dem. c.1716; Goat in Boots c.1650; Gorges House dem. 1720; Lindsey House 1630, rebuilt 1675; Manor House (Henry VIII's mansion)1536-1750; Monmouth House c.1500-1835; Park Chapel 1718; Petyt School 1705; Rectory rebuilt 1650; Rose Inn c.1720; Shrewsbury (Alston) House 1530, distillery 1730, dem. 1813; Shaftesbury House 1672-1856; Stanley House (Brickhills) rebuilt 1690; White Horse c.1670; Winchester House 1662-1830; World's End c.1670.

Society at the age of 25, and two years later he became a Fellow of the Royal College of Physicians. An appointment as Physician to the governor of Jamaica led to his early study of tropical plants, and when he returned to England he brought a number of specimens with him which he presented to the Physic Garden at Chelsea. His career as a physician blossomed – Queen Anne and George I were among his patients – and he was made Physician General to the Army; in 1719 he was elected President of the Royal College of Physicians and in 1727, President of the Royal Society.

At his home in Bloomsbury he amassed a huge collection of books, natural history specimens and other souvenirs of his travels. Although his property interests in Chelsea were growing (he had bought More's old home, the near-derelict Beaufort House, in 1736 and demolished it), he did not move with all his possessions into the Cheyne house until 1742. Thus, the great collection which was to form one of

the nuclei of the British Museum, was housed in the mansion used previously by Henry VIII's discarded wives and children. By then Sloane was over eighty, a widower and an invalid, and thinking of the end. His dream was to see the house become a permanent museum to display his antiquities, books and works of art. He bequeathed the house and the collection to trustees, instructing that both should be offered to the country for the nominal sum of £20,000, the condition being that they should all be kept together in one place, in or near London, and exhibited freely for public use. Horace Walpole was scathing in his comments on the Sloane bequest and in his evaluation of it in a letter written in Februry 1753, only a few weeks after Sloane's death, wrote that Sloane "valued it at four score thousand and so would anybody who loves hippopotamuses, sharks with one ear and spiders as big as geese."

Parliament ungraciously accepted the bequest, but decided to house the collection and other treasures

31. *Principal buildings of East Chelsea 1630-1750. The Bun House c.1700-1839; Chelsea Pensioner c.1800; Chelsea Waterworks 1722-1853; Don Saltero's 1695-1867; Drummer Boy c.1780; Duchess of Mazarin's house 1685; Gough House 1707-1960; Physic Garden 1673; Radnor (Ormonde) House 1730; Ranelagh House 1690-1805; Rotunda 1742-1802; Royal Hospital 1682; Royal Hospital inn c.1750; Ship House 1669; The Swan c.1600-1780; Thomas Franklin houses 1700; Walpole House c.1690;*

that had become available in the mansion that belonged to the Duke of Montagu in Bloomsbury – now rebuilt as the British Museum. The old house in Chelsea was demolished in 1755.

Sloane was buried in the graveyard of Chelsea Old Church. His memorial, a simple stone urn, survived the Blitz and stands to commemorate his life and his death in 1753 "with conscious serenity of mind" at the age of 92.

Chelsea manor was subsequently divided into two. One portion went to his daughter Sarah, wife of George Stanley of Paultons in Hampshire, and the other to her sister, Elizabeth, wife of Baron Cadogan

of Oakley, a descendant of the Welsh prince, Cadwgan ap Elystan. Eventually much of Chelsea was concentrated in the ownership of the Cadogan family, and this is reflected in the many street names featuring personalities and places mentioned above. Other Cadogan names and seats included Culford, Ixworth and Tedworth.

F.P. Thompson's map of Chelsea, 1836, is dedicated to the third Earl Cadogan. It shows development in the central and northern sections (with the large exception of the Brompton Park nurseries), where only sixty years earlier cows had grazed on Chelsea Common.

Tasteful Trades

THE CHELSEA PORCELAIN WORKS

Chelsea's association with porcelain, pottery and decorative tiles goes back over three centuries, in this country only rivalled by the wares of Bow as competition for the ceramic art of China. In the late seventeenth century, East India companies were importing Chinese porcelain to Europe, as well as tea, and by the reign of Queen Anne its acquisition was a feverish fashion among ladies in society. "China is the passion of her soul", wrote John Gay.

Porcelain, such as that originating in the Far East, was distinguished from stone and earthenware, its utilitarian counterparts, not only by its fine design and ornamentation, but by its translucence. Stoneware was being produced nearby in Fulham in the 1670s by John Dwight, who claimed to have "created something resembling porcelain", but this could not be compared with the items produced at the Chelsea factory which was situated approximately at the corner of Lawrence Street and Justice Walk in the mid 1740s, and which today is commemorated by a plaque.

Thomas Faulkner attributes the establishment of the Chelsea china factory to a Belgian, Nicholas Sprimont, who began his career as a silversmith. He was joined in the enterprise by a friend, Sir Everard Fawkener, Secretary to the Duke of Cumberland, and they leased an old timberyard and workshops near a riverside wharf where clay could be unloaded.

The production involved complicated moulding, firing and glazing, which made Chelsea porcelain among the most famous and highly prized. The early ware had a warm and mellow glaze into which the coloured decoration sinks rather than lying on top. Collectors look for slight faults, warping, or crazing in the glaze, and when held to the light the pin-prick holes which help to identify genuine specimens.

The first plain white jugs, in which the base is in the form of two recumbent goats, were marked with a simple incised triangle, the word 'Chelsea' and sometimes the year of manufacture. Some of these

32. Monmouth House at the north end of Lawrence Street, in a part of which Nicholas Sprimont, owner of the Chelsea Porcelain factory to the left, lived 1747-69.

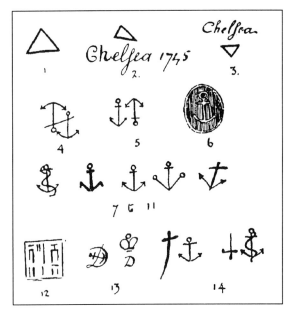

33. *Marks on Chelsea china.*

jugs were also decorated with a raised bee, giving rise to their description as 'Goat and Bee'. Other early specimens featured the shapes or decorations of sea shells and sea creatures, such as crayfish.

William Duesbury, a skilled modeller and artist, produced a series of birds. Some of the figurines provide a unique visual record of the passing scene in rural Chelsea – they portray fishermen, gardeners, flower sellers and watermen. Then there were 'Chelsea Toys', pretty little knick-knacks, snuff-boxes, scent bottles and pill cases in the shape of hearts, flowers, cupids, or other doll-like figures.

Dishes were often made in the shape of huge vegetables or animals. The 1755 sale catalogue describes a tureen in the shape of a hen with chicks, "as big as life.... set in a curious dish adorned with sunflowers".

The factory provided employment for a large number of local people. When in 1759 Sprimont appealed to the government for some protection against foreign imports, he said that the factory had not only "been set up with great labour and large expense, being as good as Dresden", but was employing "at least a hundred hands with thirty lads from parish and charity schools".

The corpulent Sprimont became a wealthy man, riding about London in a gilded cabriolet, with a country home in Dorset and handsome houses in Chelsea and Richmond. In 1756 William Duesbury left London and set up his own business in Derby, which was eventually to become the famous Crown Derby factory.

Sprimont's failing health was undoubtedly the reason for the sale of the Chelsea stock and works in 1769. It was bought by James Cox, who very soon afterwards resold to Duesbury, who then combined production with that of his Derby factory. However, output in Chelsea was less and by 1771 it was said that there were then only seven employees and a horse operating the machinery. Duesbury closed the works in 1783 and retired to Derby. Within a few years the site had been cleared to build houses, but at various times since there have been discoveries of the remains of kilns and fragments of the wares which brought so much fame to these early craftsmen.

The manufacture of ceramics in Chelsea did not cease with the closure of the Chelsea Porcelain factory. At much the same time Josiah Wedgwood took a site stretching from Upper Cheyne Row to Kings Road (where Glebe Place is now) to build a small factory in which to decorate pieces manufactured at his works at Etruria, in Staffordshire. Among the most famous items produced here was the dinner service made in 1773 for Catherine, Empress of Russia, for her palace at St Petersburg. No less than 800 pieces were decorated with views of English stately homes and their occupants.

THE GREAT TILER

William de Morgan, master potter, designer and artist left a legacy of delight. His association with Chelsea began in 1872 when he moved to 8 Cheyne Row (now no. 30), where his neighbours included the elderly Thomas Carlyle. De Morgan was 33 and already under the spell of the famous 'Firm' of William Morris, Marshall Faulkner & Co, for which he was designing stained glass. It was while experimenting with this that he accidentally discovered the ancient Islamic technique of producing lustrous metallic glazes. He built a kiln in the garden of his Chelsea house where he was able to produce his own tiles as well as decorate them. In 1876 he enlarged the business, taking a lease on the Orange House (on the site of the Church of Our Most Holy Redeemer). The coach house next door was used for a larger kiln, with his two assistant painters, Charles and Frederick Passenger working on the floor above. Part of the building also provided a showroom. De Morgan always shared the tasks, even the elementary ones, himself, and it was at this time that he was experimenting again with lustres which Minton's had shown at the 1851 exhibition when he was a boy.

In 1887 de Morgan and his factory moved out to the rapidly developing industrial area on the Fulham riverside, near the newly-built Wandsworth Bridge. Here he did some of his best work, including the tiles for 8 Addison Road, the home of Sir Ernest Debenham,

34. William de Morgan.

35. An advert for the de Morgan Company.

36. A set of de Morgan tiles, vase pattern.

and those in the Arab Hall in Lord Leighton's house in Kensington.

The de Morgans were then living in delightful seclusion at The Vale, in a rambling house decorated with art nouveau creations of himself and his friends, but in 1908 this backwater was redeveloped and they and the other inhabitants staged an elaborate 'house cooling' party before going their separate ways.

For de Morgan it was to 127 Old Church Street, Chelsea where he continued the new career which had already supplemented his ceramics – that of novelist. His first book *Joseph Vance*, of Dickensian type and proportions (230,000 words), was a best-seller.

De Morgan died in Old Church Street in 1917. The Fulham factory was demolished after the Second World War to build council flats, but de Morgan Street remains as a memorial to a man who created much beauty there.

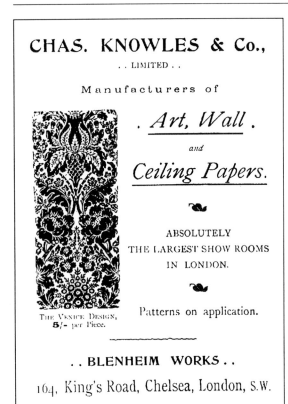

CHAS. KNOWLES & Co.,

. . LIMITED . .

Manufacturers of

. *Art, Wall* .

and

Ceiling Papers.

ABSOLUTELY
THE LARGEST SHOW ROOMS
IN LONDON.

Patterns on application.

THE VENICE DESIGN,
5/- per Piece.

. . BLENHEIM WORKS . .

164, King's Road, Chelsea, London, S.W.

37. *The 'Cadogans' were also served by the largest showroom of wallpapers in London, Charles Knowles at 164 Kings Road.*

ROUND THE MULBERRY BUSHES

In 1718 Mr John Appletree took out a patent for an "undertaking to manage and produce raw silk of the growth of England and to raise a fund for the carrying on of the same". His mentor was a retired surgeon-major, Henry Barham, who had settled in Chelsea and who decided its situation was ideal for the cultivation of mulberry trees on which to breed silk worms. He was not the first to attempt this. Mulberry growing is recorded at Syon House in 1548, and James I attempted it in the grounds of today's Buckingham Palace.

When the Raw Silk Company was launched with a large authorised capital, there was fast and furious investment in it. The site chosen for the scheme was the 32 acres known as the Sandhills, once part of Thomas More's estate, bounded today by Kings Road, Fulham Road, Park Walk and Old Church Street.

The product was said to be very rich and beautiful, but within less than three years the novelty of the venture was wearing thin and the crash came in April 1724, when the company went bankrupt. It is sug-

gested that this was caused by a mistaken planting of black mulberries as well as white ones – only the latter are attractive to silkworm larvae; or else the free-trade policy of Robert Walpole, which had removed tax on raw silk from Europe, was responsible.

The trees remained as the area became developed, and some survive today as a reminder of that enterprise.

CHELSEA BUNS

A Chelsea Bun should be a special delight, but today it is often no more than a slightly upgraded 'penny bun'. Although made in the traditional whirled shape, it is far removed from its early description of a "zephyr in paste, fragrant as honey and sweeter in taste.... as flaky and white.... soft and doughy and slight...."

In the early eighteenth century, when the Chelsea Bun became a popular novelty, the recipe was a rich one. It consisted of yeast dough enriched with eggs and butter, seasoned with lemon rind and spice, particularly cinnamon, but not necessarily the currants we expect now. The shape was obtained by rolling up the dough and cutting it across in thick slices which were then baked cut-side uppermost,

38. *The trade card of Richard Hand of the Chelsea Bun House.*

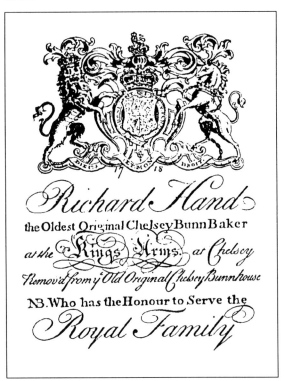

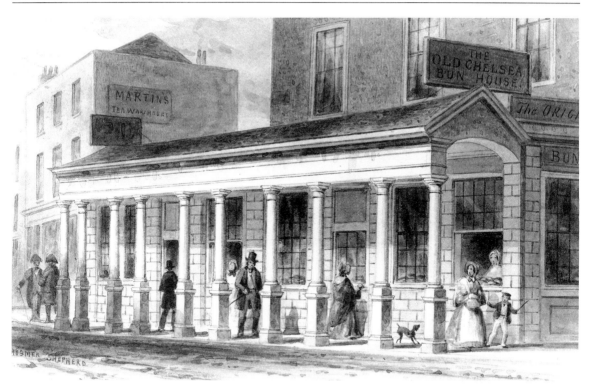

39. *The Chelsea Bun House, depicted in* The Mirror, *1839.*

40. *The interior of the Bun House depicted in the same year.*

close together (to give the moist doughy sides), and liberally sprinkled with sugar.

This was the sort of bun undoubtedly produced at the Chelsea Bun House. However, despite its name this establishment was, strictly speaking, outside the parish boundary, being situated in Jews Row (now Bloomfield Place) just off the end of Pimlico Road, but no history of Chelsea ignores its Bun, nor its football club – also outside the boundary!

The Bun House was run for four generations by a family called Hand. It was a long single-storey building with a colonnaded front (similar to those in the Pantiles, Tunbridge Wells). This gave protection to the customers queuing to buy. Dean Jonathan Swift was one of those in 1712; he was not very satisfied with his purchase, as he recorded in his *Journal to Stella*. "It cost me a penny and was stale!"

He must have chosen an off day, for the buns were extremely popular, even with members of the Royal Family in Georgian times. George II, his queen and the princesses often honoured the Hand family with their presence; and Queen Charlotte, consort of George III, presented the Mrs Hand of the time with a silver mug, which was proudly displayed. On Good Friday mornings, when hot cross buns were also sold, the crowds grew so large that Mrs Hand had to issue a notice in 1793 that she would not be selling anything other than the ordinary Chelsea Buns in order not to harm her good relations with her neighbours, who were distressed by the apparently riotous mob.

The proximity of Ranelagh Gardens gave an extra boost to trade, but even as late as 1829, by which time Ranelagh was derelict and nearby fields were a Cubitt building site, the Bun House, it was said, sold nearly a quarter of a million buns on Good Friday. Just over ten years later the old Bun House was demolished, and although a new building replaced it the area had lost its charm. In 1951, during the Festival of Britain, a replica of the Bun House was set up in Sloane Square.

BOX FARM AND THE PHEASANTRY

Box Farm was on a site later taken by the Classic Cinema. Its owners sold greens and milk to local residents, but in 1865, Samuel Baker, its owner, was advertising in the magazine *The Field* that those interested in pheasants should visit no. 152 Kings Road, next to Box Farm.

In 1881 the Pheasantry had new occupants, the Jouberts, well-established cabinet makers and decorators. They were one of a number of fashionable firms moving into the 'Cadogans' where hundreds of rooms were ready and waiting for fine furnishings. Within months, the frontage of the Pheasantry had been suitably Frenchified and its interior turned into salons and showrooms. Probably the most remark-

able member of this family was Felix Joubert, who was not only an architect, but a craftsmen who could turn his hand to almost anything from sculpture to jewellery. In the 1920s, at the instigation of Sir Edwin Lutyens, he made miniature furniture, picture frames, fencing armour and other items for the famous Queen Mary's Dolls' House.

The family also went into building development – Joubert Mansions and Joubert Studios in Jubilee Place. By the early part of the First World War, the Pheasantry building was let as studios, and only the basement was kept as workshops. When Felix decided to retire in 1932 the management of the property was taken over by an Italian, René de Meo, who founded the famous Pheasantry Restaurant and Club (see p132).

MR JONES COMES TO TOWN

In 1877 Peter Jones, a Welsh draper, took over nos. 4 and 6 Kings Road. He had come to London ten years earlier and after an apprenticeship had saved enough to acquire two shops in Draycott Avenue which opened as a 'Co-operative Drapery'. It was while the two shops were being knocked through into one that the building collapsed, killing an apprentice and burying Mrs Jones in the debris. She survived, and the shocked Jones and his few assistants recovered. The shops were rebuilt and within a few more years he had moved to the Kings Road near Sloane Square between a boot shop and a grocer.

As was often the case with drapers of that period, thriving on the seemingly inexhaustible appetite of the Victorians for drapes and furnishings, Jones gradually extended his line of shops until it reached twelve, with 200 employees. In 1884 he decided to rebuild. There arose an edifice of red brick and stone, with a green slate roof, considered magnificent at the time. The inside was "lighted by electricity", and

41. The rear of Box Farm in the Kings Road.

42. The present Peter Jones building in Sloane Square, designed by William Crabtree.

the departments were furnished with walnut and ebony show-cases and decorated with potted palms. Deliveries were made to the local terraces by nine vans, drawn by pairs of horses stabled in Rawlings Street. Jones, remembering his own days as an apprentice, behaved considerately to his younger staff – their hostel had a library, piano and billiard tables, and the food was good.

In 1903 Peter Jones fell ill and the business, so much under his personal care, began to go downhill. He died in 1905 and the year after it was up for sale at £22,500. Mr John Lewis, another Welsh draper of renown in Oxford Street, put the money in cash in his pocket, caught a bus to Sloane Square, and bought it. In 1914 Lewis handed over control of his shops to his son Spedan, who developed the 'partnership' system for which the company is famous, in which staff have a financial stake in the profits of the firm.

The old store in Sloane Square was replaced in 1932 by a building which excited much admiration in architectural circles. It was designed by William Crabtree in steel and glass, which gave "the impression of lucidity and taste".

MORE POTS

The Chelsea association with ceramics was perpetuated in modern times by David Rawnsley, a former film art director, who established the Chelsea Pottery in 1952 at 13 Radnor Walk where Buchanans had made hand-pushed milk floats for over a century. An Open Studio where pottery was taught was combined with a commercial operation producing a wide range of hand-made ceramics. The technique used to produce the new Chelsea look was sgraffito, where the decorative designs were incised into the wares before the colourful glazes were applied.

Both sides of the business flourished with a substantial export trade. When Rawnsley died in 1977 the Pottery was continued by Brian Hubbard, who remains a consultant with directors R.J. and C.M. Dennison.

The pottery remained in Radnor Walk until 1994, when sadly it had to make way for redevelopment. It is now not far away in Ebury Mews, Belgravia, where the business still thrives.

43. *Ranelagh Gardens c1764, showing the Chinese House, the Rotunda, and the Company in a Masquerade.*

Pleasure Gardens

ROGUE RANELAGH

When the Irish peer Richard Jones, 3rd Viscount and 1st Earl of Ranelagh, was appointed Paymaster General of the new Chelsea Hospital in 1685 (see p.26), he decided to build himself a handsome house in its grounds.

Despite his successful career as Chancellor of the Exchequer and Vice Treasurer of Ireland, he had a roguish reputation, and this was soon to be confirmed when he began to milk the Hospital funds for his own advantage. Described by a contemporary as a "man of great parts and great vices, a person who loved his ease and his belly and all sorts of pleasures and most profuse therein", he was on the verge of bankruptcy when he received the Hospital appointment. It was not surprising that tongues wagged when there arose a handsome brick mansion nearby on which the historian John Bowack thought "his Lordship had spared neither labour nor cost." He added that, "The very greenhouse and stables adorned with festoons and arms have an air of grandeur not seen in many princes' palaces."

Despite the rumours, Ranelagh was able to clear himself of corruption and he was even granted all the land he occupied in perpetuity. This consisted of twenty acres, much of which he laid out with lavish gardens, with agreeable walks, pools, statues, rare orchard trees, an aviary and a 'bathing house'. However, his chicanery eventually caught up with him, and in 1702 he was found guilty of gross fraud of £72,000 and forced to relinquish his post, though managing to hold on to his property. Swift described him as "the vainest old fool that ever lived but he was a clever old fool for all that."

The Ranelaghs continued to maintain their social status. After her father's death his unmarried daughter, Lady Catherine Jones, lived in the house and on the evening of 22 August 1715 entertained George I and leaders of London society there. On one of the flotilla of illuminated boats which conveyed the guests to Chelsea, Handel conducted a 50-strong orchestra in a performance of his *Water Music*.

RANELAGH GARDENS

Ranelagh House and its grounds were acquired by a consortium headed by Lacy, the patentee of Drury Lane Theatre, in 1733. The intention was to convert them into a pleasure garden to rival Vauxhall Gardens. However, little was done until 1741, when a new company, headed by Sir Thomas Robinson, renowned for the length of both his countenance and his speeches, began work on the construction.

44. A view of the interior of the Rotunda, painted by Canaletto.

45. An invitation card to an event at Ranelagh Gardens.

The centrepiece was a magnificent amphitheatre, the Rotunda, designed by William Jones, architect to the East India Company. Constructed mainly of wood, it was modelled on the Pantheon in Rome, 185ft in diameter, with four Doric portico entrances. The interior was surrounded by a gallery, and the decorations were said to be unequalled in Europe for their beauty, elegance and grandeur.

The Rotunda opened on 5 April 1742, a month before the inauguration of the gardens. Apart from providing an indoor venue for entertainments and concerts (Mozart performed here in 1764), visitors were dazzled by the brilliant lighting, describing it as a fairyland, a giant's lantern, or an enchanted castle. In the evening the admission charge was half-a-crown (12½p), which included tea and coffee. Horace Walpole was one of those not so impressed, visiting Ranelagh soon after its opening. He wrote to a friend that "although the vast amphitheatre was finely gilded and illuminated" he still "preferred Vauxhall and one goes by water". (To reach Ranelagh one often had to make a somewhat hazardous journey by coach across the Pimlico marshes.) Walpole changed his mind a couple of years later when he and almost the whole of the rest of London went there constantly. Lord Chesterfield, for example, was said to be so fond of it that he ordered all his letters to be delivered there.

In 1749 a Jubilee Masquerade was held to celebrate the signing of the Peace Treaty of Aix la Chapelle, an occasion which Walpole described as "the best understood and the prettiest spectacle that I ever saw, nothing in a fairy tale ever surpassed it." The Masquerade included maypole dancing and various bands in fancy costumes. Gondolas floated on a canal, and all round the Rotunda were stalls and booths selling china and novelties, while the theatre itself was bedecked with flowers and greenery.

Later on, when the royal family were frequent visitors, Walpole noted that you could not set your foot without treading on a Prince of Wales or a Duke of Cumberland. Dr Johnson considered it "a place of innocent recreation", and other visitors included Goldsmith and Joshua Reynolds.

In June 1775 the Thames was turned into a floating town next to Ranelagh, and another lavish occasion was the gala given by the Spanish Ambassador in 1789 to celebrate the recovery of George III from one of his bouts of illness. The King himself was too frail to attend but the rest of his family were there. One hundred valets in scarlet, and footmen in blue and silver, waited on the company. As on many other occasions fireworks were part of the entertainment, accompanied by "the fire music composed by Mr Handel". On another evening a model of Mount Etna was constructed as a set piece for "a fiery conclusion". Thomas Faulkner recorded "that no place was ever better calculated for the display of beauty and elegance."

One of the last events marked the Peace of Amiens in 1802. The main attraction was a balloon ascent by M. Garnerin, accompanied by a Captain Snowden of the Artillery, dressed as a sailor; the balloon rose a thousand feet above Ranelagh, before drifting off to Colchester, where it made a forced landing.

And yet despite all this Ranelagh declined rapidly. It acquired a dubious reputation as a hunting-ground for prostitutes, its better-off patrons became attracted elsewhere and, in 1805, the Gardens were closed. In his *Walk from London to Kew* in 1820, Richard Phillips described the "spot covered by nettles, thistles and rank weeds and holes filled with muddy water". The mansion had been pulled down and the Rotunda demolished.

Inevitably, the site went up for sale as building land, but it was acquired eventually by the Metropolitan Board of Works and its gardens added to those of the Chelsea Hospital. The site of the Rotunda is now marked by a summer house.

CREMORNE

In 1778 Thomas Dawson bought the house known as Chelsea Farm which, thirty years earlier, had been the home of the pious Methodist Countess of Huntingdon. Created Viscount Cremorne in 1785, Dawson employed James Wyatt to enlarge and improve the house and its grounds, described as richly wooded with an abundance of noble elms.

Lady Cremorne, a great grand-daughter of William Penn and named Philadelphia in his honour, ran Cremorne House, as it was then called, with housewifely skill not usually found amongst eighteenth-century aristocratic ladies. She was much liked in the neighbourhood, patronised local tradesmen and kept her servants (her housekeeper stayed over 48 years).

On Lady Cremorne's death, the estate was bought in 1830 by a colourful character, Charles de Bérenger, self-styled Baron de Beaufain, a title as vague as his claim to be a Prussian nobleman. His plan was to establish a National Club "for the cultivation of skilful

46. *A poster advertising the attractions of Cremorne Gardens in 1852.*

47. *A balloon ascent from Cremorne Gardens; pencil and watercolour by Henry and Walter Greaves, 1872.*

and manly exercise" which included sailing, rowing, fishing, waterfowl shooting and bathing, as well as fencing, archery, riding and skating. As time went on these attractions were supplemented by more populist activities, such as fireworks, circus perform-ances, music and dancing.

When the Baron died in 1845 the estate was sold to another and more ambitious entrepreneur, Thomas Bartlett Simpson, who from humble beginnings as a waiter at a tavern in Drury Lane, was now able to raise the £6,000 needed to turn the sporting centre into the Cremorne Pleasure Gardens in the style of the now defunct Ranelagh. The new venture lasted for over thirty years and was renowned for its bal-loonists. The 12-acre grounds were filled with exotic, if rickety buildings which included a theatre and concert rooms, a large dancing area (said, rather optimistically, to accommodate 4,000 people), a maze, supper alcoves, grottos and refreshment booths.

Visitors like Whistler and the Greaves brothers were entertained by fire eaters, tightrope walkers (one managed to cross the Thames), performing animals, dwarfs, giants and unfortunate human freaks; more seriously there were mock battles and military tour-naments.

The ballooning, however, was the most sensational activity. The public were invited to make ascents in a captive balloon which rose to 2,000 feet, but on some occasions it broke loose from its mooring, as it did when it sailed as far as Tottenham with a group of freezing and terrified passengers who must have been very relieved to come down safely. On another occasion a professional balloonist was carried as far as Dieppe, and in 1846 an unfortunate monkey was dropped by parachute. A French performer, Mad-ame Poitevan, dressed as Europa, ascended on a flight with a bull which happily survived the ordeal.

In 1874 Vincent de Groof, known as the Flying

Man, attempted to descend from a balloon called 'The Czar' from a height of 500 feet by the use of huge bat's wings 37 feet wide. As the balloon drifted over St Luke's church in Chelsea he attempted an emergency landing, but crashed to his death.

Thomas Carlyle was one of the local residents who protested at the amount of noise and disturbance that Cremorne Gardens brought to the neighbourhood. As the clientele became rowdier and less socially acceptable over the years, the tone of the Gardens deteriorated until in 1877 the then owner was refused a licence.

Within months the whole area had been put up for sale – even the old elm trees were felled for the timber. The adjacent Ashburnham Park Nursery was able to expand and at least that part of the old gardens survived until the building of Ashburnham School in 1907, by which time Ashburnham Mansions already towered over the flower beds and greenhouses. The rest gave way to the rows of grey houses in dismal streets leading back to the Kings Road. An 1894 map shows the riverside lined with factories and wharves, soon to be joined by the power station.

48. De Groof falls to his death near Cremorne in 1874.

49. A remnant of the old Cremorne Gardens as shown on a postcard c.1905.

Bridge Work

THE ARTISTS' BRIDGE

Chelsea's three bridges must be the most artistically portrayed in Britain. For over a century many artists who resided in Chelsea recorded the wooden structure, towers, piers and other features of Battersea, Chelsea and Albert Bridges.

The first of them, Battersea Bridge, superseded a horse-ferry, recorded by topographer John Norden in 1592, which docked near Danvers Street. In 1618 the right to operate the ferry was granted by James I to his "dear relation, Thomas Earl of Lincoln", who in his turn leased it to William Blake, the occupant of Chelsea Park.

It was the last owner of the ferry, the Earl Spencer, who instigated an Act of Parliament in 1766 to replace it with a bridge, financed by a company of which he was a shareholder. The bridge crossed the Thames from a point 100 yards up river from the Old Church, and it cost £15,662 by the time it was completed in 1772. Designed by Henry Holland, it was made of timber, was 24ft wide, and had 19 spans. It was the first Thames bridge to have lighting, first by oil lamps in 1799, and then by gas in 1824.

Investors were rewarded by the profit from tolls, but the severe winter of 1795 did so much damage that no dividend could be paid for three years.

In 1873 the bridge was bought by the rival Albert Bridge Co., whose architect, Rowland Mason Ordish, carried out concrete strengthening of its foundations, and in 1879 it was, together with other London bridges, taken over by the Metropolitan Board of Works and freed from tolls. By then it was so insecure that in 1883 it was closed to any but foot traffic, and in 1887 it was demolished and replaced by a conventional iron bridge designed by Sir Joseph Bazalgette. But before its demise the old bridge had inspired artists such as de Wint, Walter Burgess, Frank Short, Whistler and Greaves to paint it.

Its demolition was mourned by Alfred Beaver, the Chelsea historian, who although declaring that it was "utterly detested by practical people" (its narrow spans caused many accidents), "being to them nothing but an eyesore and an encumbrance", its removal was "a sad loss to the picturesqueness of Chelsea"

The new structure, which was 40ft wide and included two tramlines, was opened by Lord Rosebery on 31 July 1890.

50. Travellers being conveyed across the Thames at Chelsea Reach by watermen, depicted by Thomas Rowlandson, c.1799

51. *Battersea Bridge, looking towards Battersea. From Dugdale's Curiosities of Britain, c.1838.*

52. *Battersea Bridge; pencil and watercolour by Horace Robert Cauty, 1885.*

53. Albert Bridge, from the Illustrated London News *in 1873.*

THE ALBERT BRIDGE

The Royal Albert Suspension Bridge, to give it its full title, has earned almost unanimous affection since it was constructed in 1873. Its leading champion in modern times was John Betjeman, who led the successful campaign to save it in the 1950s, when its frail condition and unsuitability for modern traffic caused the London County Council to threaten its destruction. He described it then as "shining with electric lights, grey and airy against the London sky; it is one of the beauties of the London river". Its designer was R.M. Ordish, who employed the patent straight chain system he had used for the Franz Joseph bridge in Prague, with the carriageway and footpaths carried from the four towers by diagonal bars.

Betjeman helped to save the bridge, but it needed drastic repairs.

CHELSEA BRIDGE

The first Chelsea Bridge, designed by Thomas Page, was built 1851-8 on what is believed to be the route of an old ford across the river. It is suggested that this is a route used by the Romans in their invasion of England, and certainly many artefacts have been discovered at this point, including a Celtic shield, which suggest that a battle took place here. It was also about here that in July 1948 a Mr Joe Simms, aged 51, a Southampton dockworker, secured himself a place in *The Times* by walking across the river with only his head above the water, claiming a new method of progress through water, using a slow cycle action, a triumph of mind over matter, to cross in 17 minutes. He also claimed that he could kneel on salt water. However, research by the eighteenth-century historian, William Maitland, records that a ford had been charted here no more than 4 feet 7 inches below the water, so Mr Simms might well have had his feet on the ground.

The structure designed by Page was a suspension bridge, built very much on the same lines as the earlier bridge at Hammersmith by Tierney Clarke. It survived until 1936, when it was replaced by the modern utilitarian version in steel and granite, designed by G. Topham Forrest and E.P. Wheeler. No one could write of this, as the *Illustrated London News* did of its predecessor in 1858, that it was "a fair structure, with its beautiful towers gilded and painted to resemble light coloured bronze and crowned with large globular lamps diffusing sunny light all around."

Up river, just over the Chelsea border, the West London Extension Railway constructed a bridge in 1863 to carry their line from Kensington to Clapham. It spanned the width of the river (706 ft) on a viaduct of arches, and was designed by Brassey and Ogilvy.

54. *Chelsea Bridge, 1852.*

55. *'The Fleet of the City Steam Boats Passing in Review Order off Chelsea on the Annual Commemoration'. Tinted lithograph by H.S. Melville, c.1859.*

Boats and Boatmen

THE NATURAL HIGHWAY

The Thames has been everything to Chelsea – a highway, work place, pleasure ground – and a great visual adornment. Its shores may change, but the river itself represents a timelessness which only the most unimaginative can ignore. This water bore Thomas More on his last voyage, heard the first playing of Handel's *Water Music*, carried kings and queens on great and fearful occasions, and inspired artists such as Turner and Whistler.

Apart from the small rowing boats and wherries that infested the river, by the mid nineteenth century steam vessels were a familiar sight. The Carlyles frequently made their journeys by water from Cadogan Pier, built for the Chelsea Steamboat Company in 1841. Among the boats were those of the Citizen line, built at Battersea and named alphabetically – the last of the fleet was *Citizen S*, over 120ft long, its name being changed to *Snowdrop* when sold to another company. These were paddle steamers.

In one of Walter Greaves' pictures he depicts a sign near Battersea Bridge which advertises 'Steamboats to the City every 15 minutes'. Such vessels also carried freight and this trade increased when the canals reached the Thames. More wharves and jetties were constructed, and horses were used cruelly for loading and unloading. Coal was unloaded at Alldin's (later Johnson's) Wharf, Chelsea for many years to avoid the excise charged by City of London porters. There were many ways of access to the Thames. There were Stairs such as Beaufort, Feather, the Old Magpie, Bishops', Hospital, Ranelagh and Yorkshire Grey, all named after local landmarks, and every pier and wharfside had its full complement of sailing barges.

THE DOGGETT RACE

The river was important in the financial viability of Ranelagh Gardens and was therefore part of people's leisure activities. There were also regattas and boat races, the most famous of which was the race for the Doggett Coat and Badge, which continues still.

Thomas Doggett (1650-1721) was an Irish comic actor who became the manager of Drury Lane Theatre. According to Richard Steele, he was "a Whig

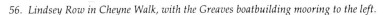

56. *Lindsey Row in Cheyne Walk, with the Greaves boatbuilding mooring to the left.*

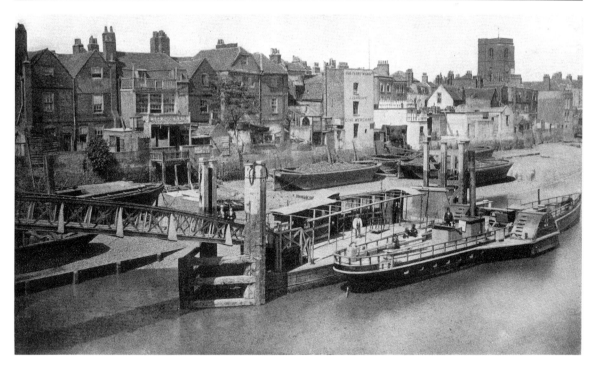

57. The riverside wharves west of the Old Church from the Arch House and Alldin's Wharf to the Adam and Eve pub (third from the left). Photograph by Hedderley in 1870.

58. The race for Doggett's Coat and Badge; as depicted by Rowlandson

59. *A livery company barge off the Old Swan at Chelsea; painting by Walter Greaves.*

up to the head and ears" who dreaded a return of
the Stuart monarchy. He instigated the race, rowed
on each 1 August, to celebrate the accession of the
Hanoverian George I in 1715. The competitors were
to be six watermen who had just completed their
apprenticeship, and the race was designed to test
their skill on the river with all its hazards. The course,
from the Old Swan at London Bridge to the White
Swan at Chelsea, near the present Swan Walk, covers
nearly five miles and the oarsmen row against the
tide, a prodigious physical effort even for tough
young men. The prize, an orange coat (the Whig
colour) bearing the white Hanoverian horse and the
badge with the inscription 'Liberty' in heavy silver,
has been replaced in modern times by a red coat and
an inscribed arm band. In the earlier days of the race
the badge weighed 12 pounds of solid silver, and
each pocket of the coat contained a golden guinea.

Doggett's will ensured that the race would continue after his death, as he appointed the Fishmon-
gers' Company as trustees. But concessions have had
to be made over the years. The heavy wherries were
replaced by Wager Boats and then Best Boats.
Nowadays the race is between what are known as
Clinker Sculling Boats and the course is from Swan
Steps at London Bridge to Cadogan Pier.

60. *Paddle steamers, yachts and rowing boats on the Thames at Chelsea in 1858.*

61. Some of the workforce of the Chelsea Yacht and Boat Company photographed during the Second World War.

CHELSEA YACHTS

The spirit of the old Chelsea waterside still reigns beneath the shadows of the Lots Road Power Station. Here are the moorings of the Chelsea Yacht and Boat Company, which since the end of the war has become one of the most interesting water-borne villages in the world.

Its foundations were laid long before housing shortages drove home-seekers to a life afloat. In 1935 the company was purely industrial – shipwrights and marine engineers carrying out overhauls and repairs. But with the outbreak of war the firm became contractors to the Admiralty, building cutters and whalers for battleships, harbour launches and lifeboats. In 1940 vessels were taken to join the 'little ships' Dunkirk evacuation.

The premises were extended to offices in Cheyne Walk and workshops in nearby Lacland Place (where previously Donald Campbell's *Bluebird* was built) and Lots Road.

The completed craft were launched locally and commissioned on the moorings where they underwent Admiralty trials prior to transportation by road to dockyards and ports. Other contracts involved the conversion of steel Thames lighters as self-propelled mobile canteens and water and fuel-carrying invasion barges in preparation for D-Day, and when completed these sailed from the boatyard to many south coast pre-invasion locations.

Although boat-building continued after the end of the war the yard undertook supplementary work on parts for pre-fab houses, the construction of 'Dragon' boats for the lake at Longleat, and sometimes the boat yard was used as a set by film companies.

When London's housing situation was acute, the first enterprising boat dwellers arrived to settle on landing craft and MTB sailing barges; these were followed by converted lighters, Dutch canal boats and even an Oxford college barge and a steam pinnace. The moorings were threatened by the proposed Motorway Box inner ring road in the 1970s, and then by the Western Environmental Improvement route, the happily unsuccessful attempts to drive an urban motorway through Chelsea.

Once these schemes had met defeat the time was right for a major reconstruction of the boatyard. The moorings were rearranged and increased, new mains services were installed, and access to the houseboats improved.

Waterworks

From medieval times London had a shortage of fresh water and problems with the disposal of sewage. When Henry VIII built his riverside mansion at Chelsea it is thought that a conduit was laid to it from the springs in Kensington, and the owners of other great houses were always eager to share such an amenity.

Although Chelsea lay between two streams, water supply was still limited, as they were drawn upon all along their courses, so that by the early eighteenth century waterworks and pumping stations, using mill techniques, were being set up to draw water from a larger source – the Thames.

In 1723 the Chelsea Water Works Company was incorporated. The engine house was actually outside the parish boundary, on the east bank of the Westbourne beside the canal leading to Belgrave Basin, approximately the site which was to become the Grosvenor Canal. The mill-like building was constructed from material salvaged from the rebuilding of St Martin-in-the-Fields church. From here the Thames water was pumped to two reservoirs, one in Hyde Park and the other on the later site of Victoria Station. At this time the main conduits were made of hollowed tree trunks from which smaller lead 'quills' took the supply to individual houses.

Tobias Smollett, who was living in Chelsea about this time, was unimpressed by the product, describing the Thames water thus drawn up as "impregnated with all the filth of London and Westminster, of which human excrement is the least offensive".

The Company made an effort to purify its product. In 1746 the first iron main pipes were laid between the pumping house and Hyde Park, and experiments began in filtering, a costly exercise which was probably the reason the company was unable to declare a dividend for over forty years.

The fierce competition between the London water companies drove them to an arrangement in 1811 to share out the London districts so as to avoid duplication, though this was of little help to areas where supplying them would be unprofitable. Experiments in filtering continued, and they were much needed. According to a pamphleteer in 1827, "the water taken up below Chelsea Hospital and London Bridge was charged with the contents of more than 130 common sewers as well as the drainings from dung hills, refuse from hospitals, lead, gas and soap works." (A white lead factory was situated only yards from the Chelsea Works.)

It was not until 1852 that reservoirs within five miles of St Paul's had to be covered, or that water from the Thames had to be taken above Teddington, but it was not until the Metropolitan Water Board, which took over the London water companies, that uniformity of quality was achieved. Meanwhile the Chelsea company had moved up river to Kingston and West Molesey, and their London land was taken by builders. The old reservoir and the lower part of the Grosvenor Canal became a refuse-loading wharf for the City of Westminster. From here much of Westminster's refuse goes by river out to sea, but at the time of writing the Council has initiated moves to try to close this wharf, sell the site for redevelopment, and send the refuse by road instead.

62. *The Chelsea Waterworks in 1752, with the marshes of Pimlico and Westminster Abbey in the distance.*

More Streets, More Churches

Opinions vary as to the architectural merit of James Savage's St Luke's, Sydney Street, but no one can deny that with its high-pitched nave, perpendicular flying buttresses and 142ft tower, in such a spacious setting, it must be one of London's most impressive parish churches. The decision to build came only after years of agonising indecision between a costly repair and expansion of the Old Church or the provision of a new one. Nothing very much happened after the decision to build St Luke's was taken by the Vestry in 1806, though urgent action was necessary even if just to provide more space for burials – the old churchyard was full, and the little graveyard in Kings Road, given to the parish seventy years of so earlier by Hans Sloane, was already inadequate. In 1810 the Vestry was permitted to take land in Sydney Street for a new burial ground and it was on this that the new church was built.

James Savage's building was one of the first of the Gothic revival churches of London, and its cost was a prodigious (for those days) £40,000. The foundation stone was due to be laid in October 1819 by the Duke of Wellington, but he was unable to attend and the ceremony was performed by his brother, the Rector of Chelsea. The consecration ceremony, which took place almost exactly five years later, included a glittering assembly of the fashionable residents of Chelsea and members of the Cadogan family.

Names associated with this church include Charles Dickens, who married Catherine Hogarth here in 1836, and the composer John Ireland, who served as organist from 1904 to 1926.

HOLY TRINITY

Soon after the building of St Luke's, Savage was working on another Chelsea church – Holy Trinity in Sloane Street, where the new Hans Town development was attracting hundreds of new residents. Consecrated in 1830, its first vicar was a curate from St Luke's, the Rev. H. Blunt. The building did not endure – it was described by Alfred Beaver in 1892 as a "melange of Gothic items of various periods" and it was very adversely criticised even at the time of its construction. Sixty years later it was replaced by a magnificent arts and crafts building designed by John Dando Sedding, a disciple of John Ruskin. The building confirmed the architect's belief that a church should "be wrought and painted over with everything that has life and beauty – covered with men, beasts and flowers...."

Certainly, everything of beauty was lavished on it. Its east window, designed by Burne Jones, was made by William Morris's company, and the interior decoration incorporated alabaster, red and green marbles and semi-precious stones, onyx, porphyry and amethyst, and metal work by Henry Wilson, Sedding's assistant.

The church weathered several incidents during the Second World War, but expensive repairs threatened its survival afterwards. No wonder that John Betjeman leapt to its defence in 1974, composing an elegant plea for its preservation in a leaflet illustrated by Gavin Stamp, which contributed greatly to the success of the campaign. In his words, "the tall red house still soars upwards to the stars".

A RASH OF CHURCHES

While affluent members of society patronised St Luke's and the earlier Holy Trinity, other churches were being built in less fashionable streets. Christ Church was opened in Caversham Street off Flood Street, then one of the main shopping areas, in the 1830s. The simplest of plans was used, although the cost of its construction was borne by the Hydman family whose wealth derived from sugar plantations. No choir stalls were provided – the singers sat in the front rows of the gallery – but a handsome pulpit was donated by a City church, St James Garlick Hill, due for demolition, as was the organ, which came from St Michael Queenhithe. The architect of Christ Church, Edward Blore, had a high reputation and his simple and traditional design had much of the old Georgian

63. The second Holy Trinity, Sloane Street; from the Builder 6 October 1888.

64. *St Luke's, the new parish church for Chelsea; from Metropolitan Improvements (1828).*

65. St Simon Zelotes church.

66. Park Chapel was built near Chelsea Park in 1718 at the expense of Sir Richard Manningham. Although it served as an adjunct to the parish church, it remained privately owned. Its ministers included John Owen, in 1812, who played a part in the founding of the British and Foreign Bible Society. It was his son, Henry John Owen, who succeeded him in 1822, who became the first minister of the Catholic Apostolic Irvingite Church in Elystan Street, Chelsea, in 1835. The Irvingites were followers of the Scots minister, Edward Irving, a friend of Carlyle, who was dismissed by the Church of Scotland for his unorthodoxy, but believed he was divinely inspired. Park Chapel was closed in 1913 .

feeling, but this was changed by alterations at the turn of the century by W.D. Caröe.

An engraving of 1855 shows the church of St Jude to be a Norman-towered building. It was erected by an Anglican congregation in Jews Row (Pimlico Road) at about that time. Its history is vague and it closed in 1932, the building demolished and the parish amalgamated with that of Holy Trinity, Sloane Street.

The church of St John in Tadema Road was consecrated in 1876. It was destroyed in the bombing of 1940, and remained derelict until the site was used for housing, although worship continued at St John's Mission Hall (built 1875) in Blantyre Street.. Today's St John's, with St Andrew's, lives on in the modern church on the World's End Estate.

The *Illustrated London News* in 1859 congratulated the Rector of Chelsea on the opening of another church in 'Upper Chelsea', this time St Simon Zelotes in Milner Street. It is a simple ragstone building designed in gothic style by Joseph Peacock. St Saviour's, on the north side of Hans Place was built *c*.1840 with "no particular pretensions to architectural effect", having no spire, only two dwarf towers flanking the Walton Place entrance. When the fate of Holy Trinity, Sloane Street was being debated in the 1970s it seemed that St Saviour's might be sacrificed in a merging of parishes, but it also gained the affection of John Betjeman who might, at first, have been deterred by its plainness. Now, however, it has succumbed to decay and it was closed in the spring of 1996; it is to be converted into a small chapel and flats.

ROMAN CATHOLICS

In the 1860s Roman Catholics in the western part of Chelsea were served by a Catholic Mission set up in Cale Street by the Order of the Servants of Mary, the Servites, and which was sufficiently successful to be made into a Catholic parish of its own. At first, worship took place in private houses in Park Walk and Netherton Grove, and a school was established on a site that was later to become part of St Stephen's Hospital. The church which resulted from these efforts was the Servite Church of Our Lady of Seven Dolours, just outside the parish boundary, designed by Joseph Hansom who, apart from being a competent architect, was the inventor, or so he always insisted, of the horse cab which took his name. The stained glass was produced by W. Tipping of Edith Grove, the organ was the work of Henry Jones of Fulham, and the west front was designed by W.H. Palmer, an architect and sculptor from Flood Street. In the 1960s parts of the decorative frontage were found to be dangerous and were removed, leaving the church a plainer building than when it opened.

On the other side of Chelsea in Cadogan Street a small Catholic chapel had been founded during the Napoleonic Wars for French prisoners billeted in the area; this was also used by Catholic inmates of the Royal Hospital. This chapel was established by an émigré priest, Abbé Voyaux de Franous. Faulkner saw the place as a saviour of poor Irish veterans "from the grossest ignorance, profligacy and vice". In 1877 it was replaced by the church of St Mary, a large but plain building, designed by J.F. Bentley.

When the Roman Catholics in the vicinity of the riverside village decided to build a church in Cheyne Row in the 1890s, the first idea was for a domed edifice on the lines of the Brompton Oratory, but the site, which had formerly been de Morgan's pottery studio, was too small and money was too short. In the end the architect, Edward Goldie, settled for a Wren-style building which upset many people who thought it more in keeping with a concert hall or, even worse, a dissenters' chapel. When opened in 1905 it was dedicated to Our Most Holy Redeemer, but after Thomas More's canonisation in 1935 his name was added to the title. On the altar is a relic from his vertebrae, which came from the convent in Bruges where his adopted daughter, Margaret Clements, became a nun.

What is thought to be the site of Thomas More's house (in Beaufort Street) is now occupied by a Convent of the Order of Adoration Reparatrice, where the nuns pray night and day for the return of England to the Catholic faith. Every year on 6 July, the anniversary of More's execution, a pilgrimage takes place with a Solemn Mass at the church followed by a procession to the convent and later, by boat, on the river to the Tower.

THE METHODIST CONNECTION

Prominent in Chelsea in the mid eighteenth century was the Methodist evangelist, Lady Huntingdon, whose followers established the 'Lady Huntingdon Connection', a splinter group of traditional Methodists. Sometimes known as the 'Queen of Methodists', she and her husband, Theophilus, had a villa known as Chelsea Farm on the West Field near Hob Lane, which led from the river to World's End, in 1740. During her life the Countess founded no less than sixty chapels in various parts of the country.

John Wesley visited Chelsea very early in his career after his return from America, and was invited to preach in the parish church of Chelsea.

An early Methodist group met for worship in the home of a Mrs Day in Upper Hospital Row, in a 'dancing room'. In 1813 a local minister who was in sympathy with the Countess's beliefs fitted up a room as a chapel in the remnant of Ranelagh House and after five years the much enlarged congregation moved to a new building in George Street, off Sloane Square, on the site of a former slaughter house. This new Ranelagh Chapel, 'a neat building', was taken over in 1843 by English Presbyterians until they themselves moved on to Halkin Street in the 1860s. Soon afterwards the old chapel was converted into the Court Theatre, forerunner of the Royal Court.

The Methodists, meanwhile, had built a commodious new chapel in Justice Walk, with a large school room below, where Queen Victoria once attended a class meeting. The congregation here included Peter Jones the draper, and Thomas Carlyle who was interested in the work for children. Early this century the church moved to the corner of Manor Street and Kings Road, but this building was badly damaged during the last war and only part of it was saved for Methodist use. In the 1970s the site was redeveloped after a fund-raising scheme (supported by Margaret Thatcher – a Chelsea resident) raised £1 million to

67. Ranelagh Chapel, south of Sloane Square, later used by the Court Theatre.

build a new church and pastoral centre, plus 21 homes for the elderly. The foundation stone was laid by the Speaker of the House of Commons, George Thomas. The premises are also used as a daily Drop In Centre, offering advice and affordable refreshment, and other facilities for elderly and homeless people.

NON-CONFORMISTS

Another wartime casualty was the church of St Columba's in Pont Street, built in 1884 for Scots Presbyterians. This was destroyed in 1941 and not replaced until 1954 by the present starkly simple building, with its facade outline of the saint with his crane bird beside him, designed by Sir Edward Maufe. Despite the bombing the congregation was kept together by the Minister, Dr R.F.V. Scott, whose responsibilities extended to the many Scots servicemen in London during the war. He was succeeded by another famous Scots cleric, the Very Rev. Dr Fraser McLuskey.

The Congregationalists built a chapel in Markham Square in 1860. Designed by John Tarring, it was a large and imposing building in Kentish ragstone, with a 130ft tower and spire. It was demolished in 1953, mourned as a 'landmark' by the Chelsea Society.

All the traditional non-conformist denominations have had to face a reduction in congregations in post war years – a number have survived by amalgamation. The present Edith Grove Christian Centre is a good example of ecumenical partnership. Its roots are in 1867, when the West Brompton Congregational Church was opened and for over seventy years was a thriving church. The building was destroyed during the war, rebuilt in 1954, and for the next five years a few members of the original church still living in the area were joined by a group which had previously met in the London City Mission in Lacland Place, closed to make way for the Cremorne Estate. In October 1960 the Chelsea Congregational Church in Edith Grove was opened, taking the name of the former church in Markham Square, and when the Congregationalists and Presbyterians merged into the United Reformed Church in 1972 the name changed again. In November 1988 there was further concentration in the building when the Chelsea Baptist Church was invited to share the premises; today there is a thriving non-conformist centre.

Until the last years of the nineteenth century a small and unpretentious chapel existed in Glebe Place, latterly used by an independent congregation. It had originally been a place of worship for Chelsea's considerable Huguenot community, led by Jean Antoine Cavallier, the leader of the Camisards in their struggle against the Revocation of the Edict of Nantes. He died in London in 1740.

THE MORAVIANS

Chelsea is particularly identified with one religious sect. It is said that it was while worshipping with a group of Moravians that John Wesley "felt his heart strangely moved", and although he did not become one of the 'still brethren', he remained sympathetic to them, writing to a friend many years later saying that "truly they are wise in their generation".

When the Moravians came to Chelsea in 1750, this group of mid-European Protestants was already well over 300 years old. Formed at the end of the fourteenth century in Bohemia and Moravia in opposition to the dogmas of Rome, they had a history of persecution and were driven from their homeland, first to Poland and then to Saxony. It was in the latter that the 200-strong group sought the help of Ludwig, Count von Zinzendorff, who had already set up his own Christian community on his estate there in 1722. It was the Count who bought for them Lindsey House, the Chelsea riverside mansion, when the group decided to come to England.

The intention was to create a self-sufficient community based on simple Christian beliefs, to be known as 'Sharon'. Buildings were to be erected in the grounds as workshops and dwellings, as well as a manse, chapel and burial ground. The latter were on the site of Thomas More's old private chapel and stables. In the burial ground, just as in the living quarters, segregation was observed, not just by sex, but between single and married people. (Contrary to popular legend, interments were not vertical to allow for speedier resurrection on the Last Day!)

The scheme was short lived, for Zinzendorff died in 1760 and money ran out. The community had no alternative but to sell off the land for building and Lindsey House itself was divided into four separate dwellings, one of which was occupied in the early 1800s by the tunnel and bridge builders, Mark and Isambard Kingdom Brunel.

68. *The Moravian Chapel in the grounds of Lindsey House.*

69. *Lindsey House, Cheyne Walk, a property bought for the Moravians when they first arrived in Chelsea.*

Among the most prominent of the Moravians were James Hutton (1715-1795), a friend of John Wesley, and James Gillray, father of the caricaturist of the same name. Gillray senior, an old soldier and Chelsea out-pensioner, acted as sexton for forty years. It was Hutton, a former bookseller, who had to arrange for the transfer of the group to a more modest home in Pimlico, although the chapel remained open for worship, as it does to this day. Modern congregations have a strong Caribbean element, reflecting Moravian missionary zeal in the West Indies.

An exhibition centre was opened in 1982 and can be seen by appointment.

Parts of the old stables are now studios, which have been occupied by artists and the photographer-historian, John Bignell. The burial ground survives and is one of the most attractive secret corners of old Chelsea.

A QUAKER IN CHELSEA

There is no record of a Friends' Meeting House in Chelsea, although it was the home of a renowned Quaker, Edmund Howard, steward and friend of Sir Hans Sloane, as well as being a faithful diarist of contemporary life. Howard acted as caretaker of Beaufort House between Sloane's purchase of it and

its demolition. In the end Sloane gave him the unenviable task of demolishing the house and then Howard moved in to a lodge near the Moravian church where he established a herb garden and a collection of rare plants.

Living with him was his brother, a skilled clockmaker who made the clock for the Old Church in 1761 at a cost of £50, and placed a clock face on the lodge frontage which gained it its name of The Clockhouse (not to be confused with the Norman Shaw building on the riverside). The Howard clockhouse was pulled down in the mid nineteenth century.

OLD BURIAL GROUNDS

Few people realise that behind a high wall in Fulham Road, near the Queen's Elm, there is a quiet resting place for the many Jews who lived in London in the early nineteenth century, the land having been bought by a Jewish society in 1813.

Another early burial ground, that of the Roman Catholic church of St Mary in Cadogan Street, was closed for burials in 1958, when thirty acres in Kensal Green Cemetery were bought for Catholic interments.

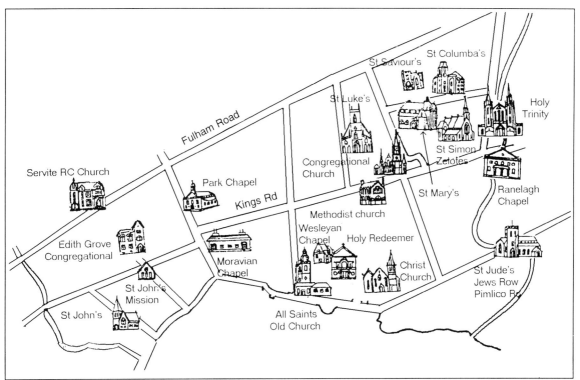

70. Chelsea Places of Worship. Servite R.C. Church 1874; Edith Grove Congregational (now Christian Centre) 1867-1941, rebt. 1954; St John's, Ashburnham Road 1876-1940; St John's Mission Hall 1940-76; Park Chapel 1718-1913; Moravian Chapel 1753; St Luke's 1824; St Simon Zelotes 1859; St Columba's 1884, rebt. 1954; Christ Church 1839; St Jude's, Jews Row (Pimlico Rd) 1855; Holy Trinity, Sloane Street 1828, rebt. 1890; Congregational church, Markham Square 1860; Methodist Church, Kings Road 1900; Wesleyan Chapel, Justice Walk 1841; St Mary, Cadogan Street 1882; Holy Redeemer R.C. Church, Cheyne Row 1895; Ranelagh Chapel 1819-43. Then Presbyterian, then Court Theatre; St Saviour's, Walton Street 1840.

71. The Old Clockhouse.

People of Politics

POLITICAL PENFRIENDS

Although it is to literature that they first belong, both Joseph Addison (1672-1719) and Richard Steele (1672-1729) were politicians in the broadest sense, using their skill as journalists to influence the opinions of the time. Of the same age and from the same school, Charterhouse, their careers ran in tandem for a number of years and they were near neighbours in Chelsea. Addison's sojourn at Sandford Manor on the banks of Chelsea Creek might technically be considered to make him a Fulham resident, but the boggy estuary of the stream made boundaries vague. This was the time when he was courting the widowed Countess of Warwick at Holland House and writing letters on the natural history of the area to her young son.

At the same time Steele, with his beloved wife Prue, was living at Cheyne Walk and he and Addison shared cheerful meetings at Don Saltero's coffee house there (see p75). Steele had founded *The Tatler* in 1709 to publicise his Whig views and soon too Addison was a contributor; In March 1711 *The Spectator* was begun, with a famous series of essays by them both, which appeared daily for 555 issues until December 1712.

72. Joseph Addison, from a portrait by Dahl.

73. Sir Richard Steele, an engraving from a painting by Godfrey Kneller.

The fortunes of both of them changed after the death of Queen Anne and the accession of George I. Steele was re-elected to parliament and knighted, but had money troubles and quarrelled with Addison. Addison married his Countess and moved to Holland House, but he died young, aged only 43.

DR ATTERBURY

"An ambitious and turbulent priest attached to the House of Stuart", was how Horace Walpole described Dr Francis Atterbury, Jacobite politician, preacher and theologian, who was living in Old Church Street from about 1685, when he was fined for not keeping his river wall in repair (his exact address is not known). At this time he was in political favour, Queen Anne having appointed him Bishop of Rochester. However, his correspondence with the Old Pretender, James Stuart, the only son of the exiled James II, roused anxious suspicions in Whig circles and in 1722, at the time of the Jacobite rebellion, Atterbury was sent to the Tower and later exiled for the remainder of his life.

74. Dr Atterbury.

JONATHAN SWIFT

The best-known political writer for the Tories was Dean Jonathan Swift who, during their brief spell of government in 1710-14, produced *The Examiner*, and it was during this time that he wrote his *Journal to Stella*, a series of letters in which he expressed his views of the times. In the summer of 1711 he spent a few months in Chelsea, in rooms in Old Church Street, where he was not pleased to find that his neighbour was Atterbury. However, despite their political differences, Swift was pleased to accept the tasty meals that Mrs Atterbury sent to his lodgings where he complained of having "a silly room with coarse sheets" for which he had to pay six shillings a week.

The future author of *Gulliver's Travels* didn't much like Chelsea anyway. He found it tedious to make the journey to visit his friends in London, and complained that local residents showed their "cunning" by taking up all the stage coaches, and there were no boats on Sundays. Even the "hay making nymphs" were "perfect drabs in dirty straw hats". He left in July that year and never came back to stay.

A REFORMING MAGISTRATE

Not strictly a politician, the Bow Street magistrate Sir John Fielding, was, however, something of a social reformer. In the mid eighteenth century he and his half-brother, the novelist Henry Fielding whom he succeeded as magistrate, carried out a number of innovations which altered the lives of many Londoners.

Sir John lived for a time in one of the portions of Monmouth House at the top end of Lawrence Street, where he was a neighbour of Tobias Smollett. It may have been in his honour that Justice Walk was named, although there may also have been a court house there on the site of the later Wesleyan chapel.

Despite being blind, Sir John was much aware of the social conditions of the period and was particularly concerned at the plight of young boys brought before him, forced into crime by poverty. He was responsible for the first patrols of the Bow Street Runners, the earliest London police force.

A PRIME MINISTER IN RESIDENCE

The title of 'Prime Minister' was neither official at the time nor intended as complimentary when it was applied to the Whig politician, Robert Walpole (1676-1745). It was used instead by his detractors to signify his dictatorial attitude and his power over his party, but there is no doubt that this short, fat (he weighed 20 stone) Norfolk squire served his country well, with great wit and wisdom during the early decades of the Georgian era.

For twenty of those years he spent his summers at Chelsea and it was to Walpole House, to the west of the Royal Hospital, that everyone who was anyone

75. Jonathan Swift.

76. Sir John Fielding.

77. Sir Robert Walpole, from the painting by J. Van Loo.

in politics came. His son Horace, who was hardly more than a toddler when the family came to Chelsea, grew into manhood there and was to become one of the most pertinent chroniclers of the age.

Robert Walpole was already intimate with Chelsea, having been Paymaster of the Royal Hospital in 1714. In 1721 he took the house which had been built in 1687 by William Jephson, and set to work enlarging it; the 4½ acre garden, which included a large greenhouse, summerhouse and orangery, was laid out by Sir John Vanbrugh.

Walpole did not get on with George II, though he was friendly with the ill-used Queen Caroline of Anspach, and it was she and her children that he entertained at Walpole House in August 1729, with music playing from barges on the river and guests parading through the elegant rooms of the house.

The house was later bought so as to build a new infirmary for the Hospital, though some fragments of it were incorporated into the new building.

A RADICAL MAN

One of the most controversial politicians of the nineteenth century was Charles Dilke, born in 1843 in the house, 76 Sloane Street, in which he spent most of his life. He inherited a family tradition of interest in social reform and when he entered Parliament in

Gladstone's second ministry he became Under Secretary of Foreign Affairs. Three years later he was appointed President of the Local Government Board, reflecting his interest in franchise reform, and he seemed destined for the highest office in the land.

But in 1885 this apparently respectable politician, married to the daughter of an Army captain, was cited as a co-respondent in a much-publicised divorce case. He strenuously denied culpability, but his parliamentary career was ruined.

OTHER NOTABLES

Sylvia Pankhurst (1882-1960) campaigner for women's rights, lived at 120 Cheyne Walk, where a blue plaque has been erected. Karl Marx was at 4 Anderson Street for about two years before being evicted for non payment of rent in 1851. William Wilberforce lived at 44 Cadogan Place for the last three weeks of his life, within days of the success of his Anti-Slavery Bill. The Macmillans, parents of Harold Macmillan, were living at 52 Cadogan Place when he was born in 1894. It was to this house that their son returned after being severely wounded on the Somme battlefield. A successor to Macmillan in Downing Street was Margaret Thatcher, who clung to her 19 Flood Street home for some years after taking office. Doubtless it will have a blue plaque in time.

Stories out of Schools

THE PARISH SCHOOL

The local historian, John Bowack, attributed the large number of boarding schools for young ladies in Chelsea to "the sweetness of the air and the pleasantness of the situation". Certainly Chelsea was healthy but it also had a large number of substantial houses suitable for schools. Even before the time of Bowack's description this was so. In the *London Gazette*, 25 November 1680, an advertisement appeared: 'Josias Priest, dancing master, who kept a boarding school for gentlewomen in Leicester Fields, is removed to the great house at Chelsea at which was Mr Portman's, there will continue the same masters and others to the improvement of the school.'

Mr Portman had presumably been a tenant (probably also a schoolmaster) of Gorges House. It was here in 1690 that Mr Priest's pupils gave the first performance of Purcell's opera *Dido and Aeneus*, with one of the girls, Lady Dorothy Durk, speaking the special epilogue.

There was also a parish school in Bowack's time. In 1705 Chelsea Vestry authorised William Petyt, lawyer and Keeper of the Records at the Tower of London, to rebuild and repair at his own expense the old parish school which was by then established a hundred years. The new building, in Old Church Street, was also to provide a vestry room where the affairs of the parish could be considered. Despite the rebuilding the new school was quite small, only 28 x 26ft.

Its chief purpose was "the education of poor children in the knowledge and practice of the Christian religion as professed and taught in the Church of England." The schoolmaster had to "frequent Holy Communion, govern himself and his passions, write a good hand, understand the grounds of arithmetic, and keep good order in his own family". Though he had to enforce discipline, he was not allowed to whip

79. *Petyt's Charitable School, as depicted in 1829.*

children except in the presence of one or more of the governors or trustees who had "the power to hear and examine the crime and remit the punishment". The children were obliged to attend church twice on Sundays and at the end of the service line up with their caps off as the congregation emerged. They were also bound to greet any of their benefactors by doffing their caps and bowing.

Among the most generous benefactors of the parish school was Luke Thomas Flood (d.1860), after whom Flood Street is named. His gifts included rewards for academic prowess and punctuality, as well as payments for apprenticeships, bread and clothing.

By 1819 over a hundred boys and girls were being clothed and educated free. The girls then moved to a house in Lordship Lane endowed by the Rector, and finally in *c*.1825, when new schools were built in Kings Road, the Petyt School building was used as a 'fire engine house' until it was too dilapidated, when it became a mission hall. Finally, it was demolished in 1890 but rebuilt in replica as a Church House. This was destroyed during the last war and was rebuilt as a parish centre.

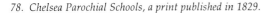

78. *Chelsea Parochial Schools, a print published in 1829.*

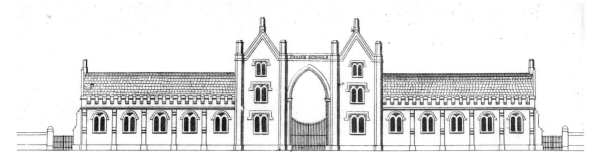

NATIONAL SCHOOLS

In common with other parishes, Chelsea had some National Schools – establishments run by the National Society in collaboration with the parish churches, in which the pupils were brought up in the principles of the established church. The first of these was attached to St Luke's (1829) and the second to Christ Church off Flood Street – the latter still survives as a Church of England Primary School.

A school for "very poor children" was formed in 1819 through the generosity of a builder called Whitehead, who was responsible for a number of streets in the Chelsea Common area, including the 'Grove' named after him. A print depicting his school shows a substantial three-storey house which accommodated 124 boys and 75 girls, all taught according to the National Society system. For non-conformists, there were British Schools attached to Ranelagh Chapel.

As a result of the 1870 Education Act, which established local Boards of Education, Chelsea was linked with Fulham for administrative purposes, and in the next ten years schools such as Ashburnham in the west of the parish, and Marlborough in the east were established.

FOR THE NAVY AND THE ARMY

Ormonde House at the east end of Paradise Row was taken in 1777 as a Naval Academy. A pamphlet dated October 1781 described its situation as "being truly on the banks of the Thames in a fair healthy detached spot. It is an old house, properly cleansed and fitted up to contain 28 scholars with several officers and servants." The proprietor was John Battesworth, who taught mathematics and navigation, and the Treasurer was Jonas Hanway, described as "a very benevolent gentleman best remembered in connection with the introduction of the umbrella." More significantly, Hanway in association with Sir John Fielding and others, founded the Marine Society aimed at training young and destitute boys for service at sea.

In the Chelsea academy all pupils had to have either already suffered smallpox of have been inoculated against it. Entry was at the age of eleven when they were sworn in at a quaint ceremony repeated on their leaving three years later, enjoining "religion, peaceableness, good humour, purity of speech and discipline". In 1782 a model ship was erected in the grounds and christened with due ceremony 'The Cumberland', in honour of the Duke, who was the

80. The children at their lessons in the Royal Military Asylum; by Pugin and Rowlandson, c.1808.

81. The Royal Military Asylum, a print published in 1805.

82. Jonas Hanway.

school's president. Mounted on a swivel base it provided rigging on which the boys could carry out naval exercises.

In 1801 the government bought a large site on the south side of Kings Road to build the Royal Military Asylum for the children of soldiers of the regular army. The foundation stone of this grand building, with its Doric portico, was laid by the Duke of York, brother of the Prince Regent. Most of the thousand or so children were orphans, others had fathers abroad, some were just from large, poor Army families. The boys, in red jackets, blue breeches and stockings and black caps, had military training; the girls, in red gowns, blue petticoats and straw hats, learnt domestic skills for them to use as servants.

The girls were moved to a similar institution in Southampton in 1823 so as to enlarge the capacity in Chelsea for boys. In 1909 the school moved to Dover, with some of the grounds sacrificed to a widening of Kings Road, and by 1911 the building was taken over by the Territorial Army as the Duke of York's Headquarters, a use which has continued to the present, with the grounds providing playing fields for a variety of clubs and schools as well as Army sports teams. Bannister and Chataway and many other famous athletes trained here.

Although Louis Lochee's Military Academy was geographically just over the border in Kensington, his association with Chelsea is too great to leave him out, for he owned much property in Little Chelsea in the 1770s. Lochee, a romantic character who specialised in military fortifications, set up his training school for young officers on a piece of land, probably between the south side of Fulham Road and backing on to the present Hollywood Road. He built model fortifications in the grounds and it was here that in 1784 an ascent was made by two balloonists, Blanchard and Sheldon. Lochee died in mysterious circumstances when he became involved in a nationalist rising in his native Belgium in 1791.

ACADEMIES

The house used in the seventeenth century as a clinic by the quack doctor, Bartholomew Dominicetti, at 6 Cheyne Walk, became a school when it was taken by the Rev. Weeden Butler *c*.1785. Butler's elder son became headmaster of Harrow School, and his younger son assisted Thomas Faulkner in his *History of Chelsea* by translating the Latin inscriptions on the church monuments as well as supplying "some philosophical and moral reflections".

A part of Monmouth House in Lawrence Street was used as a boarding school run, by a Mrs Pilsbury, in 1815 for a short time. For about forty years from the early nineteenth century Gough House to the west of Chelsea Hospital was a girls' school run initially by the widow of its former owner, and then a boys' school run by a Dr Wilson.

At Turret House in Paradise Row, a "handsome, square, brick structure built in the reign of Queen Anne", the Rev. William Rotherey ran a school "where young men were boarded and qualified for university or business". Fees were £25 for board and learning with extras for fencing, and an additional £5 for a single bed if required. In 1735 Rotherey was appointed Lecturer at the Old Church where his sermons were criticised for being "too long and not delivered with any peculiar skill." At the end of his life he became "insolvent and lost in drink."

A refugee from the French Revolution, the handsome M. St Quentin must have set the hearts of his young female pupils a-flutter when he taught them French, history, geography and "as much science as he knew" at the school run at 22 Hans Place in 1798. The girls had some serious competition, for he eventually married one of the teachers, Miss Rowden. Among the pupils here were Mary Russell Mitford, the novelist, author of the popular *Our Village* series and *Rienzi*, and the poet and journalist Letitia Landon.

In Smith Street, facing Burton Court, was an old building known as Ship House which Reginald Blunt understood had once been occupied for a year or so by Sir Isaac Newton while he was proof-correcting his *Principia*. It was rebuilt in the early nineteenth century and used as a school to teach French to about fifty boys, "sons of, or nearly related to nobility".

STRICTER REGIMES

The Hans Town School of Industry for Girls was founded in 1804 to train young girls for domestic service. Nevertheless this was less formidable than the well-meaning Elizabeth Fry's School of Discipline in Paradise Row, founded in 1825, where 42 "refractory girls were reformed for five shillings a week and trained to earn an honest living." The school later moved to Fulham but Alfred Beaver notes in 1892 that girls "still retained their ugly dress adopted by the foundress with their hair plastered down on their heads, ugly shoes and quaint aprons."

83. Elizabeth Fry.

HILL HOUSE

Until the admission of its best known pupil – Prince Charles – in 1956, Hill House school was probably best known to the general public for its crocodiles of little boys in ginger plus-fours and jerseys seen moving about in the vicinity of Hans Place.

Founded in 1951 by Colonel and Mrs H.S. Townend in Switzerland, it also took up premises a few months later in Chelsea. It became the first school to teach in two countries at the same time and with the same boys and girls in both countries, on the theory that children should be educated on an international basis. Colonel Townend commutes between the two schools weekly and is now assisted by his son, Richard Townend and his daughter-in-law.

Nowadays Hill House has over 1,000 pupils between the ages of three and fourteen, and 120 full-time teachers.

NEW STATE SCHOOLS

In 1895 the South Western Polytechnic in Manresa Road decided to set up two secondary schools for children between the ages of eleven and sixteen, the Sloane School for Boys and the Carlyle School for Girls. These were taken over by the London County Council in 1914, which moved them to Hortensia Road. In the later 1960s Sloane was caught up in the controversy over comprehensive education and feelings ran high. It was eventually closed, merged with three other schools, and became part of the purpose-built Pimlico Comprehensive.

COLLEGE DAYS

Whitelands College in Putney, a training institution for teachers now part of the Roehampton Institute, has a curious early history. About 1760 a large house next to the Royal Military Asylum in Kings Road was taken as a school. In 1842 it was bought by the National Society to establish Whitelands College as a training school for women teachers. Though it undoubtedly had serious intent, it was also known for the traditional May Day Queen celebrations held among its students, which were instigated by John Ruskin. The College moved to Putney before the last war and a block of flats on the site records its name.

The National Society also bought Stanley House in Little Chelsea in 1839 to establish St Mark's training college for schoolmasters, its principal being the

Rev. Derwent Coleridge, son of the poet. It was he who proposed that a children's school should be added, so that the potential teachers had something to practise on.

This was situated in the unusual eight-sided Octagon building next to the Chapel on the Fulham Road boundary, and provided places for 260 children.

In 1923 the College was merged with that of St John's Battersea and later moved to Plymouth, the Chelsea site being used by the King's College conglomerate until the changes of the 1980s. The old practising school building, however, continues as the private Octagon School for boys and girls, aged three to thirteen, set up by a group of parents with the aid of a charitable foundation.

THE POLY

"If only the opportunity for innocent recreation and useful instruction were provided without offensive patronage and irritating restrictions, thousands of working lads and young men would avail themselves of it." So Sidney Webb wrote in 1882 in support of Quintin Hogg's pioneer work to establish polytechnics. One of the results of this work was the formation of what became Chelsea College in 1901.

Quintin Hogg had been working among the homeless boys and shoeblacks of London since the 1860s, when he opened the Regent Street Polytechnic in 1882. When given the opportunity for a similar

84. The May Queen ceremony at Whitelands College in 1904.

85. Domestic training for young women at the Chelsea Polytechnic at the end of the nineteenth century.

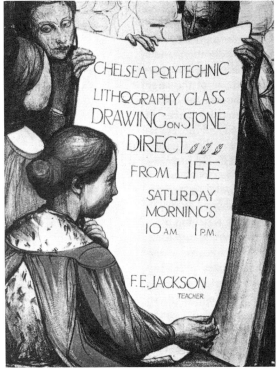

86. A poster advertising lithography classes at the Chelsea Polytechnic.

establishment in Chelsea the Commissioners of the Chelsea Public Library raised the sum of £10,000 to obtain a matching grant from the City Parochial Charities. A site in Manresa Road was presented by the Earl of Cadogan and J.M. Brydon designed the building.

Though the foundation stone was laid in 1891, due to lack of funds the building was not finished until 1896. In its early days the South Western Polytechnic, as it was then known, gave courses in science and domestic economy, training for work in factories or engineering shops, or "preparation for colonial life". During the First World War many of the senior students and all the staff worked voluntarily to make novocaine and beta-sucaine, which were used as anaesthetics in war hospitals. The carpentry rooms were utilised to make splints, and experiments were carried out to find substitutes for petrol, "Mrs Hughes testing them on the road in her motor".

In 1922 the name was changed to Chelsea Polytechnic and courses were expanded to include such subjects as pharmacy and chiropody. After the war the School of Art went independent, but even so the expansion of courses and pupils' caused serious problems with accommodation. These led to the demolition of Manresa Road's jumble of buildings and a grand redevelopment, fronted by the fire station on Kings Road.

In 1966 moves began to establish the College as a School of the University of London (a Royal Charter was granted in 1971), and from 1968 the College

began negotiations to form a link with St George's Hospital Medical School at Tooting – eventually it built a substantial campus at Springfield in Wandsworth. In 1985 Chelsea College became part of King's College which plans to dispose of the Chelsea site. At the moment the Chelsea campus includes a Hall of Residence – Lightfoot Hall – facing Kings Road, which has accommodation for almost 200 students.

THE ART STUDENTS

The present Chelsea School of Art is the result of an amalgamation of two art schools, one, as we have seen above, part of the Chelsea College, and the other the West London School of Art in Great Titchfield Street. Traditionally, both schools were inclined to the fine arts, and this has continued.

The principal of the Chelsea school from 1910 until 1958 was H.S. Williamson, who appointed such teachers as Henry Moore, Graham Sutherland and Ceri Richards.

The average enrolment of the present school is 200 full-time students and there are also evening classes. It is accommodated in one of the new buildings of the 1970s development in Manresa Road.

87. *Poster advertising what was at first called the South Western Polytechnic, in Manresa Road.*

Gardens and Gardeners

THE PHYSIC GARDEN

In 1673 the Apothecaries' Company, seeking a suitable piece of land on which to build a boat house for their state barge, leased a riverside site from Charles Cheyne on a 61-year lease at a rent of £5 per annum. Soon after its acquisition the Apothecaries established a herb garden there, the intention of which was to discover, cultivate and study the nature of plants for scientific and medicinal purposes. This continued in a modest way for nearly fifty years until it was raised in status by the patronage of Sir Hans Sloane.

That century had seen a great revival in medical botany, which had been in the doldrums since the break up of the old monastic gardens. According to John Evelyn, Physic gardens had been established at Magdalen College, Oxford and at Westminster. In 1685 he was particularly impressed by the installation of heating stoves beneath the conservatory floors at Chelsea. Sir Hans Sloane was an enthusiastic supporter of the venture and to make it secure he granted the Apothecaries a perpetual lease at a nominal rent of £5 a year on condition that each year fifty new specimens, dried and preserved, should be contributed to the Royal Society until a total of 2,000

was reached. Sloane was also instrumental in the appointment of Philip Miller as Gardener in 1722 and it was during his brilliant stewardship, lasting nearly fifty years, that the Garden's reputation was established as the finest in the country if not the world. Joseph Banks began his botanical studies under Miller's tuition, and one of his assistants was William Aitken, who later became one of the first managers of Kew Gardens. It was visited by the 'Father of Botany', Carl von Linne (Linnaeus) in 1736. Plants and seeds were received from various institutions in Europe and the Middle East, such as the four Cedars of Lebanon which were to become a famous feature of the Garden for many years. These were only 3ft saplings when first received in the seventeenth century, but they developed a girth of over 12ft before the last of them died in 1904.

During the nineteenth century the Garden encountered problems not only from the expansion of London, but the intrusion of the Embankment and pollution from nearby factories and railways, which made plant cultivation difficult. Money was short and the Apothecaries had other demands on their resources as medical botany declined in importance. Crisis point was reached in July 1890 when it was rumoured that the Society was contemplating selling off the land for building. A protest meeting was held in Chelsea Town Hall and a resolution passed to take measures to preserve the Garden. Among messages of support was one from Whistler.

Eventually, in return for government assistance, students from the Royal College of Science at South

88. The Apothecaries' barge houses and the Swan brewery; painting by G. Lambert, c.1857.

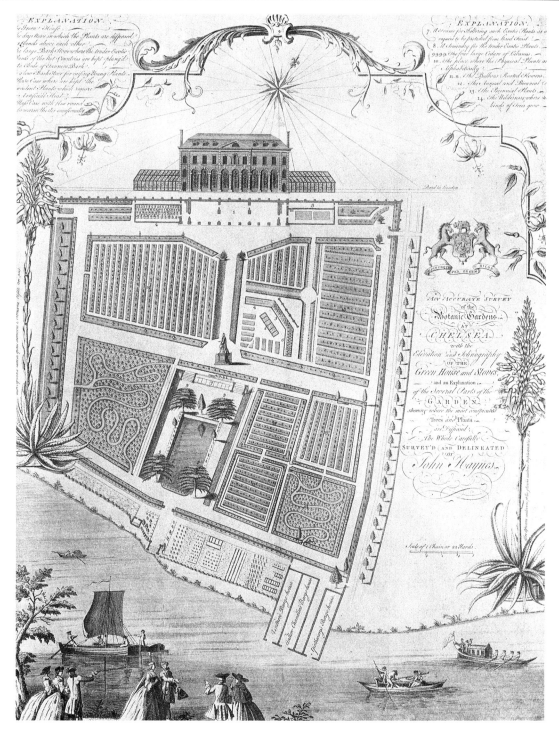

89. *Plan of the Chelsea Physic Garden, drawn up by John Haynes, 1751.*

Kensington were permitted to use the Garden. Re-organisation and a new layout followed, but it was not until 1953 that the huge botanical library at Apothecaries' Hall was moved to Chelsea.

Another crisis over the Garden's future arose in the 1970s and a new trust was set up in the early 1980s which should ensure its survival, and which has resulted in the Garden being much more accesssible to the public.

Today, the Garden's wide scope includes the bio-chemistry of plants, their world-wide cultivation, and the production of synthetic alternatives.

THE FLOWER SHOW

Chelsea's association with gardening was perpetuated in comparatively modern times by the decision of the Royal Horticultural Society to move its famous annual Show to the grounds of the Royal Hospital. The Society itself had Chelsea roots for it was William Forsyth, one-time curator of the Physic Garden, who helped to inaugurate it. In May 1912, when the Show was first held in Chelsea, the attendance was 178,389.

There are perennial threats to move the Show elsewhere because of the congestion within and without the grounds, but the atmosphere of Chelsea would be difficult to replace. The huge marquee is set up around the memorial obelisk and the red-coated pensioners mingle with the huge crowds looking at gardens which are created in a few days, and which disappear even faster.

MONEY ON TREES

In 1748 a "young gentleman of good estate and honourable position" advertising for a wife offered, as a special inducement, that her home would be in Chelsea "midst the floral beauties of the Kings Road".

For some reason this highway became the centre of horticultural enterprise during the reigns of William and Mary, Queen Anne and the Georges, when the English garden was really coming into its own. Travel and exploration were opening the eyes of gardeners to the beauties of tropical plants and the hope of adapting them to English weather.

Among the most popular businesses was Joseph Knight's Exotic Nursery at Little Chelsea, occupying a large area between the Kings and Fulham Roads. The nursery, opened in 1808, was an immediate success. Each year Knight travelled to Europe to buy plants, as well as commissioning collectors who went further afield, to Australia, Brazil and China. The *Gardener's Magazine* wrote glowing accounts of his striped camellias, a hybrid magnolia and orange trees, though it scolded him for not keeping his potting sheds warm enough for his staff.

In common with most of the other Chelsea nurs-erymen, Knight had a reputation for the thorough, though strict training of young gardeners, and among those who learned his trade under his watchful eye was Michael Rochford of the family which is still a household name in the production of houseplants.

Knight died in 1855 worth "an abundant fortune", soon after his nursery had been sold to James Veitch, grandson of a famous Scots nurseryman. The young Veitch improved the Chelsea enterprise so that it became a Victorian version of a modern garden centre. Among his collection of plants was a *Magnolia fuscata*, "trained like a peach tree so as to scent the whole of the Kings Road from end to end with delicious perfume like pineapple and some Arabian spices." Under the Veitch family the nursery attained the status of a fashionable store, the foremen wearing frock coats and top hats so as to be smart enough to conduct distinguished visitors around.

When James Veitch's grandson, Harry, retired in 1914, the nursery closed. Its site consisted of 2½ acres with frontages on Kings Road and Hortensia Road.

An earlier establishment than the Exotic Nursery was James Colvill's nursery, which began in 1783 on two grounds, one at the corner of Blacklands Lane and the other just beyond Sloane Square. By 1811 the nursery was known for its cut flowers, including the chrysanthemum from China, which Colvill had introduced in 1795. From 1819 to 1826 the foreman in charge of exotica at Colvill's was Robert Sweet, author of *Hortus Londoniensis*, a series of highly-regarded plant catalogues. Unfortunately, he was arrested for "feloniously receiving" some plants stolen from Kew Gardens, and although found not guilty he left Colvill's to retire to a private life of writing.

The last of the great Chelsea nurserymen was William Bull who acquired the business of Edward Weeks in 1860. His speciality was pelargoniums such as Chelsea Gem, and his annual orchid display became one of the sights of London. When he died in 1902, the business was given over to the manufacture of its speciality products, Bull's Fumigating Compound and Plant Food at 536 Kings Road.

Not all the nurseries were entirely commercial, nor confined to the Kings Road area. In 1789 the Quaker botanist, William Curtis, moved his garden from Lambeth to near the Queen's Elm, Brompton, and in 1798 went into partnership with an equally skilled gardener, William Salisbury. This business later moved to six acres between Sloane Street and Cadogan Place where the 'London Botanic Garden' was laid out on Linnaean principles of classification. This land eventually became the gardens of Cadogan Place.

This catalogue of Chelsea's gardeners is far from complete – there were numerous others, such as James Hair at Ranelagh who raised 43 varieties of pea, and John More, near Markham Square, who gave us More's Victory pelargonium.

Chelsea Eccentrics

DR PHENÉ

Of all Chelsea's eccentrics, Dr John Samuel Phené is among the most celebrated, and the 'château' he built on the corner of Oakley Street the most extraordinary of its buildings. A scholar and antiquarian, Dr Phené (1823-1912) was a pioneer of the now-accepted theory that trees purify the air in towns, and was able to convince Victorian developers to have tree-lined streets. A descendant of a Huguenot family, he spent much of his time tracing his lineage, claiming to date back to the Phoenicians. His first home was Cheyne House on the north-east corner of Upper Cheyne Row, surrounded by a large garden with many rare and interesting trees. In the grounds Phené collected his growing number of archaeological treasures which included remnants of old buildings.

The Phené family owned an estate in France which had included the Château de Savenay on the Loire, destroyed during the Royalist Vendean rising in the 1790s. Phené resolved to build a replica of this house in the midst of his curious garden as part of the development of Oakley Street, with which he was already involved.

Work began on the replica in 1901, when he was 78. The highly-ornamented edifice, though basically a Victorian villa, was five storeys high with a porched entrance, and smothered with gargoyles, beasts, birds, dragons, serpents and other grotesque creatures, painted in scarlet and yellow with gold embellishments like a gigantic and rather grubby wedding cake.

Phené didn't actually live in the house, preferring to be at 32 Oakley Street, where by now he had designed many more conventional houses as well as those in Margaretta Terrace (named after his first wife). A short, dapper little man, with a Vandyck beard, he became a recluse, sitting alone in his eerie monumental garden, safeguarded by a secret lock of his own design, dwarfed by the vast statues in a tangle of undergrowth. He died in 1912 and the odd house was demolished in 1917.

JOHN SALTER

Phené's passion for collecting would have been admired by another eccentric, John Salter, who lived not a stone's throw away, but two centuries earlier. A former travelling valet to the greatest collector, Hans Sloane, his coffee house in Cheyne Walk was crammed with curios – his 'knackatory' he called it – became one of the sights of London in the early eighteenth century.

Salter had already run coffee houses in Lombard

90. Dr Phené.

91. Don Saltero's coffee house as it appeared in 1840; drawing by Alfred Beaver in 1859.

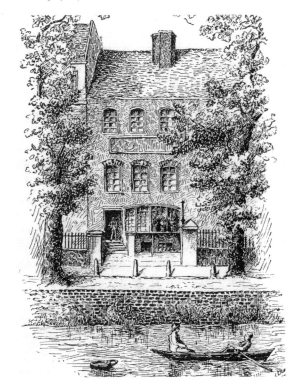

92. *Dr Phené's bizarre house in Oakley Street, up for sale.*

93. James Camden Neild; engraving from a portrait by De Wilde.

JAMES CAMDEN NEILD

James Camden Neild occupied 5 Cheyne Walk for at least sixty years from the end of the eighteenth century, gradually becoming odder and more miserly. His father, also James, was a West End jeweller who took the house in 1792, and spent his private life investigating the conditions in prisons, especially those in which debtors were confined. James junior inherited his considerable fortune, but despite this he was so mean that he refused to take a cab or use any form of transport to collect the rents of his far-flung properties. He walked everywhere in shabby, threadbare clothes. The house, which even in his father's day had been sparsely furnished, became increasingly squalid. He was said to have barely any comforts, ate meagrely and had no company but a cat, yet when he died in 1852 it was discovered that he had left half a million pounds to Queen Victoria. When the Queen conveyed the good news to her uncle Leopold he replied that it "was very good news because one never knew what might happen to Royalty which was already much diminished on the Continent."

A QUACK DOCTOR

Count Alessandro di Cagliostro, described as a "necromancer and quack of quacks", lived in Sloane Street in 1786. An Italian whose real name was Guiseppe Balsamo, he had already been disgraced abroad where he had founded a secret sect, dabbled in the occult and imprisoned for his part in what was known as the Diamond Necklace Affair. He nevertheless managed to impress gullible Londoners, advertising his Egyptian pill of life at thirty shillings a dram as well as love philtres and other concoctions. When he subsequently went to Rome he was soon put in prison, not for his dubious cures but for forming an Egyptian Masonic group and engaging in spiritualism.

OLD CHAMBERS

A lesser-known eccentric, discovered by Richard Edmonds when researching Chelsea Library archives in 1954, was 'Old Chambers', who was pilloried in a highly libellous article published in a local newspaper in 1839. 'Constant Reader' informs the Editor ("knowing his willingness to expose every species of vice") that the "old debauchee" living at 21 Camera Square, although extraordinarily rich from his ownership of numerous ground rents lived in squalor and was in the habit of hiring women at 2s 6d a night to take part in naked orgies. (Camera Square is now Chelsea Park Gardens. The name Camera is preserved in Camera Place between Park Walk and Limerston Street. The origin of the name is unknown.

Street, Danvers Street and Cheyne Row before he placed a notice in *The Tatler* in 1709, advertising himself by his new nickname of 'Don Saltero' (said to have been given him during the Spanish wars), and his collection at a new address "six doors from Manor Street" at 18 Cheyne Walk.

The weird objects on show included a "piece of Solomon's temple", "a purse made of a spider from Antigua", some "beads made from the bones of St Anthony", and dozens more.

It is not clear when Salter died, but in January 1799 the whole place was sold at auction. The curios were sold off in 121 lots, the whole proceeds of the sale amounting to little more than £50.

Women of Some Importance

MARY ASTELL

In post-war years the Chelsea Society placed a tablet on the walls of the rebuilt Old Church dedicated to four of Chelsea's many scholarly women and to honour the British Federation of University Women which had occupied Crosby Hall on the Embankment for over fifty years. Those commemorated are Margaret Roper (1505-1544), daughter and confidante of Thomas More, Magdalen Herbert, Lady Danvers (1568-1627), Elizabeth Blackwell (d.1758) whose *Curious Herbal* has become a classic botanic reference, and Mary Astell (1668-1731), a woman so far ahead of her time that she frightened male academics.

Mary Astell came to London from Newcastle equipped with an education usually reserved then for boys – her uncle, a clergyman, had taught her in mathematics, logic, philosophy, Latin and Greek. She is believed to have lived in Swan Walk (some say Paradise Row) for most of her life in Chelsea. It was in 1694 that she wrote her *Serious Proposal to Ladies for the Advancement of their True and Greatest Interest*. Mary Astell had ideas about marriage that were distinctly unorthodox. A woman could, she said, be "yoked for life" in an arranged loveless marriage and "denied her most innocent desires for no other cause but the will and pleasure of an absolute lord and master whose follies a woman cannot hide and whose commands she cannot but despise at the same time as she obeys them." Her practical solution was the foundation of an academic community of "pious and prudent women" pledged to scholarship and celibacy, where they might retire from the world if they wished. Bishop Burnet condemned her plans as "resembling a nunnery and paving the way for popish orders", but the scheme began to attract support from a number of influential and wealthy society women, one of whom had offered £10,000 towards the establishment of such an institution. Her neighbour, Dr Atterbury, confided in a colleague that he dreaded to engage in verbal debate with her so only "writ a general civil answer" to her theological and philosophic arguments. He said that he found her a little offensive and shocking in her expressions, but still of an extraordinary nature, considering they came from a woman.

In the late 1720s she developed cancer and endured the agony of surgery, spending her last days with a coffin beside her bed to "keep her mind fixed on proper contemplations." She died in May 1731.

Although her earlier dream of a women's college came to naught it did lead indirectly to the foundation of the Asylum for Soldiers' Daughters, established shortly before her death by some of her followers.

ELIZABETH BLACKWELL

A contemporary of Mary Astell was Elizabeth Blackwell, who came to Swan Walk only a few years after her death. She was a woman after Mary's heart, a strong character who managed despite the constrictions of the time to develop her talents, becoming her family's breadwinner and gaining a lasting academic reputation.

Born in 1688, she was 36 when she came to Chelsea with her husband, a Scots physician who for some reason had changed his profession to become a printer and had gone bankrupt in the process. Fortunately, Elizabeth was a talented artist and the keeper of the nearby Physic Garden was anxious to catalogue its growing collections. Thus was produced *A Curious Herbal* containing 'Five Hundred Cuts of the most Useful Plants which are now used in the Practice of Physic. Engraved on folio copper plates after Drawings taken from Life by Elizabeth Blackwell.' It is more than possible, given the medical uses of the specimens, that her husband helped her with the captions, but it was Elizabeth's fine skill in drawing and delicate hand colouring which made the book not only a reference volume, but a work of art. But while the volume was being produced the family suffered a tragedy – the death of both their children.

Alexander Blackwell, for reasons that are not clear, then went to Sweden, where he first became the Royal Physician and then became embroiled in politics. He was arrested, charged with high treason and then executed. Elizabeth survived him by eleven years, presumably still living in Swan Walk, and died in 1758; she was buried in the Old Church graveyard.

FALLEN ANGEL

"It was a story all the world knew", said the diarist John Evelyn, of the life of Hortense de Mancini, the Duchess of Mazarin, who enlivened the social whirl of late seventeenth-century London. Yet such is the short life of scandal that the lady was soon forgotten in her own time, let alone this.

Hortense in her prime was a dazzling, dark-haired blue-eyed beauty, who lived for a short time later in her life in Paradise Row. This pretty terrace of houses, with dormer windows, handsome porticoed doorways, pillared entrances and long back gardens, lined the north side of the main route leading from the Kings Road to Chelsea village and riverside until the opening of the Royal Hospital Road. She was a niece of the wealthy Cardinal Mazarin, and spent

94. Hortense Mancini, Duchess of Mazarin; from the painting by Pierre Mignard.

95. Dorothy Jordan.

her girlhood at the French court, where she caught the eye of the future Charles II of England, then in exile there. However, she was sold off to a crazy, religious fanatic of a husband from whom she fled at the earliest opportunity, after being shut up in a nunnery. Disguised as a boy, she travelled across Europe, keeping one step ahead of her pursuers until reaching the sanctuary of London at the age of 28 in 1675, where her relationship with Charles II was rekindled. A royal allowance of £4,000 a year should have kept her in comfort had her life style been more modest and her love-life more discreet, but gambling debts and scandalous liaisons took their toll, and when Charles died in 1685 she found herself in reduced circumstances. She left her apartments in St James's to retire to her 'country home' at Chelsea and the company of her faithful, if elderly admirer, the Seigneur de St Egremont, a fellow refugee whose touching devotion survived all her taunts, tantrums and vagaries of affection. He was approaching his eighties when she was in her forties, but he courted her with the grace of a man half his age. She, in fact, died before him, of drink it is said, at the age of 51. Her crazy old husband arranged for her body to be embalmed and returned to France, where he carried it around with him on his travels.

ROYAL FAVOURITES

Dorothy Bland (Mrs Jordan), the actress who had enjoyed a life of cosy domesticity as the mistress of William, Duke of Clarence, came to live for two years from 1812 at no. 3 (now no. 30) Cadogan Place. Having borne her lover no less than ten children, and helping to hold the family's finances together by her stage earnings, the unfortunate woman now faced an enforced parting from him, brought about by the command to all the sons of George III to make legitimate marriages and produce a much needed heir. William did as he was told, produced several children, but none of them survived infancy. He later became William IV on the death of George IV.

A later royal favourite, Lily Langtry (1852-1929) had several homes in Chelsea over the years, including 37 Ovington Square, 18 Pont Street and 15 Tedworth Square, which she later sold to the famous cricketer, 'Plum' Warner.

In 1882 the glamorous actress and socialite had ideas for a house in Cadogan Place to match her flamboyant life style. It was to be designed by Edward Godwin, to have five storeys facing the square garden and incorporate a palm court and studio salon. She eventually settled for a smaller place, possibly because the Prince of Wales failed to finance the plan.

96. Jane Austen; sketch by her sister, Cassandra.

97. Letitia Landon.

JANE AUSTEN

Jane Austen's association with Chelsea was transitory. In the spring of 1811, just before *Sense and Sensibility* was published, she came to London to stay with her brother and his wife at their grand house, 64 Sloane Street. Some idea of the kind of home it was is given in a letter to her sister, Cassandra, in which she describes a musical evening where the musicians arrived in two hackney carriages and a crowd of nearly sixty guests could be accommodated in the reception rooms.

Two years later her brother's wife was dead, and he moved out of Chelsea to some rooms over his bank in Henrietta Street, Covent Garden, but in 1813 he moved back to another house in Chelsea at 23 Hans Place. She was to visit him there several times before 1815 when during one of her stays he was taken seriously ill. The young doctor called to attend him was the 28-year-old Charles Haden, who had been elected to the Royal College of Surgeons at the age of twenty and had a brilliant career ahead of him. He became a friend of the family and Jane had a special regard for him.

Jane returned to Chawton when her brother had fully recovered. Two years later she herself was dead and Charles Haden had married. His son, Francis Seymour Haden, born at 62 Sloane Street, became a well-known surgeon as well as a skilled etcher, and married Whistler's half sister, Deborah.

L.E.L.

Letitia Landon, 'L.E.L.' to a generation of Georgian readers, did not share Jane Austen's lasting fame. Born in Hans Place in August 1802 to a wealthy family made less so by the South Sea Bubble crash, Letitia was sent to the school run by M. St Quentin only a few doors from her home at 22 Hans Place.

At the age of twenty Letitia had already shown considerable talent, having had her first poem, *Rome*, published as well as becoming a book reviewer. Her novels and long, romantic narrative poems became best-sellers and she was soon earning enough to support her hard-up family. Painters such as Daniel Maclise portrayed her in pink and white, and she was involved in several scandals before she married George Maclean, Governor of Cape Coast Castle in Africa in 1838 and left England to live there that year. Four months later she was found dead, an empty bottle of prussic acid beside her. It was never proved whether she committed suicide or was murdered.

MARY SOMERVILLE

Mary Somerville, wife of William Somerville, the Physician Surgeon at Chelsea Hospital in the early nineteenth century, was an academic woman of rare talent whose ability was recognised by the Royal Astronomical Society and the Geographical Society, and awarded a Civil List pension.

RADCLYFFE HALL

Scandal and sensation of a very different kind attached themselves to Marguerite Radclyffe Hall, who preferred to be known to her friends as 'John'. In 1928 she wrote *The Well of Loneliness*, the first novel to dare tackle the subject of lesbianism. The book, published by Jonathan Cape, was almost immediately withdrawn on the orders of the Home Secretary. "I would rather give a healthy boy or girl a phial of prussic acid", wrote James Douglas, editor of the *Daily Express*, than let them read it. It was not until 1949 that it was successfully republished in this country.

Radclyffe Hall lived at 22 Cadogan Court, Draycott Avenue from 1907 to 1916, and later at Swan Court and Cadogan Square.

NOVELISTS

When Vera Brittain came to live in Cedar Studios, Glebe Place in 1935, she had just written her autobiography *Testament of Youth*. (In private life she was married to George Catlin and became the mother of the politician, Shirley Williams.) *Testament of Friendship*, a memorial to her friend, the novelist Winifred Holtby, was to follow but by then she had left Chelsea. She died in 1970 at the age of 77.

98. Lily Langtry.

99. Marguerite Radclyffe Hall; photograph by Howard Coster.

Angela Thirkell (1890-1961), grand-daughter of Edward Burne Jones and cousin of Rudyard Kipling, brought Trollope's Barsetshire into the twentieth century in the 1930s and 1940s, with her novels *The Brandons* and *Northbridge Rectory*. She had homes at Cheyne Walk and Shawcross Street at various times.

Chelsea has only the flimsiest claim to any connection with Elizabeth Gaskell, who was born at 93 Cheyne Walk (Lindsey Row) on 29 September 1810 as Elizabeth Stevenson, but remained there only a few weeks owing to the death of her mother shortly after the birth.

Equally brief, but at the other end of her life, was the association with Chelsea of Gaskell's friend George Eliot, who came to 4 Cheyne Walk in October 1880, the year of her marriage to John Cross. She died three weeks later, having caught a chill while attending a concert.

A happier residence was that of Naomi Mitchison whose novels, produced over three decades from the 1930s, were amongst the most popular fiction of the time, although she was equally recognised in academic circles for her classical scholarship and as an educational reformer. She spent the first five years of her married life at 17 Cheyne Walk.

Medicine Men

PRACTITIONERS

Today, Chelsea is noted for its hospitals – the Chelsea & Westminster, the Royal Brompton and the Royal Marsden. But Chelsea's association with medicine is much older than these. From about 1639, in the house which was the forerunner of Lindsey House on the riverside, a famous Swiss doctor lived, Sir Theodore Turquet de Mayerene, who had previously served as physician to both Henry IV and Louis XIII of France, and in England to James I and Charles I. He was controversial in the use of chemistry in prescriptions, rather than herbal remedies. He spent all his last years in Chelsea up to his death in 1655; his manuscripts are preserved in the Sloane Collection at the British Museum and the Ashmolean Library at Oxford.

Another distinguished physician, Dr Richard Mead, had a house in Paradise Row (and also possibly in Cheyne Row) in 1714. Among his skills was his diagnosis of hydrophobia, although his remedy of an ash coloured moss mixed with pepper sounds rather crude. He is believed to have persuaded Thomas Guy to found his hospital, although Mead's intention was that it should be a hospice for incurables,

100. Dr Richard Mead, 1739; from an etching by Arthur Pond.

and he subsequently refused to become its president.

Among his many talents Hans Sloane was also a knowledgeable physician, and was one of the first to study smallpox inoculation. Unlike Jenner, he used the actual disease for inoculation, rather than cow-pox, sometimes with fatal results. When he helped to save Princess Caroline's daughter of the disease he declined to inoculate her other two daughters on the grounds that it was too dangerous. But she bribed six charity children to undergo the treatment and when all bar one survived, the royal children were also successfully inoculated. Sloane also used quinine for the treatment of malaria.

Smallpox inoculation was also carried out at a house in Danvers Street in the 1760s by Alexander Reid, an Assistant Surgeon at the Royal Hospital. An advertisement in 1764 announces that "the apartments are pleasant and commodious and patients are inoculated and attended with the utmost care and tenderness for ten, five or three guineas according to their choice of accommodation."

An extraordinary institution in Chelsea was established by Dr Bartholomew Dominicetti at 6 Cheyne Walk in 1766. This he converted into a 'sanatorium' to receive patients undergoing his patent medicated steam baths. He claimed to have spent over £37,000 converting the vast house, which had 13 bedrooms, four parlours and two dining rooms. He erected thirty 'sweating chambers' in the garden and four 'fumigating bed chambers'. Among his patients were the Duke of York and Sir John Fielding, but Dr Johnson ridiculed his treatment, which was claimed to cure all manner of diseases including leprosy, scrofula, rheumatism and asthma.

William Wilberforce's leading role in the anti-slavery movement overshadows his other achievements, which include his support for the Chelsea Brompton and Belgravia Dispensary, founded in 1812 in Sloane Square by the Rev. George Clark. The Dispensary sought to relieve the sick poor (but not paupers), to deliver infants and to treat women and children. Starting with an average of 1,200 patients a year, the number had increased to nearly 7,000 in the 1880s.

EARLY HOSPITALS

In 1866 a group of Chelsea residents took over Gough House in Royal Hospital Road and there founded the Victoria Hospital for Sick Children. The first medical officer was William Jenner and accommodation was provided for six children who "being afflicted by the providence of God are too often surrounded by any wretched and unhealthy influence". By 1890 the hospital's out-patients' department was treating 1,500 children a week and a new building was erected adjoining with provision for 103 beds. The hospital was moved in the 1960s to St George's Tooting.

101. The Chelsea Hospital for Women.

St Luke's Hospital in Sydney Street began as a workhouse infirmary. In her book *Rosemary for Chelsea* in 1971, Ursula Bloom described the "once red, now dirty brick, building and adjoining burial ground where old men and women in the last stages of decrepitude sat on the seats provided." St Luke's was closed in the 1970s and the site used to build the Royal Brompton and National Heart Hospital.

In 1883 the Hospital for Women was opened at 78 Kings Road and later moved to Dovehouse Street. This hospital was eventually absorbed into Queen Charlotte's at Stamford Brook.

The York Hospital, on the site of the present Guthrie Street, was established at the time of the Napoleonic Wars by Dr James Guthrie (1785-1856), where he treated amputees and other severely wounded men after Waterloo, using new methods. The hospital later moved to Chatham.

The Cheyne Hospital for Children suffering from Cerebral Palsy was founded in 1898 by Mr and Mrs Wickham Flower at 46 Cheyne Walk, with only four beds. As understanding of the disease increased the hospital developed, first as the Chelsea Hospital for Spastic Children and then to the modern Cheyne Centre, which has a world-wide reputation.

THE ROYAL MARSDEN

William Marsden came to London in 1814 to study medicine and was apprenticed to a doctor in Holborn. The story goes that when later in his career he found a desperately sick pauper girl lying in a doorway, he paid for someone to take her into their care and

102. The Victoria Hospital for Children.

was so affected by her plight that he persuaded better-off friends to subscribe towards a clinic where the poor could be treated without charge, first for out-patients only in Westminster and then in Chelsea. This led to the building of the Cancer Hospital in Fulham Road in 1862, at first in face of opposition to the idea of a hospital treating only one disease. Queen Victoria initially refused her patronage, but later relented and subscribed £100, making annual gifts of linen and pheasants.

In later years the hospital was joined by the Chester Beatty Cancer Research Institute, where the first work was carried out on radiotherapy and chemotherapy. The name of the hospital was changed to the Royal Marsden in 1954 and it now works in partnership with the Institute of Cancer Research, both at Chelsea and Sutton, making it one of the foremost centres for the treatment of the disease in the world.

BROMPTON HOSPITAL

Tuberculosis was the scourge of the Victorians – it features heavily in the literature of the period, and with good reason.

In 1841 a young solicitor, Philip Rose, was distressed that a clerk in his London firm could not get

103. The Consumption Hospital at Brompton.

admission to a London hospital to have it treated, mainly because the disease was infectious and usually fatal. There were few specialist hospitals available. Rose was well connected and was instrumental in setting up a meeting at his house in Hans Place to set up a tuberculosis hospital. Enough money was forthcoming in a year and they acquired the Manor House in Smith Street. Inevitably, the house became too small and in 1843 a site was taken on the south side of Fulham Road, just outside the parish boundary. One of the conditions of the lease was that the architect, George Basevi, should design the building The style chosen was Tudor gothic, popular at the time, and there was a *cordon sanitaire* of 100ft between the hospital and the rest of the estate. The wards were small and there was an emphasis on fresh air.

In the reorganisation of hospital facilities of recent years, the Brompton has been closed and its functions transferred to the Royal Brompton and National Heart Hospital in Sydney Street, but the old hospital chapel and the main northern buildings remain. There is a current plan for the conversion of the building into flats.

A WESTMINSTER WORKHOUSE
John Rocque's 1745 map shows what appears to be a block of institutional buildings in the vicinity of Park Walk in Little Chelsea. Ninety or so years later the same buildings are described as 'almshouses' and later still as a 'workhouse'. They appear to have been

constructed by the conversion of Shaftesbury House, occupied by the 3rd Earl of Shaftesbury *c*.1700. The house was demolished in the late 1860s when the parish of St George, Hanover Square, which had housed some of its poor in the building, erected here the Westminster Infirmary, a hospital mainly for poor people which had "modern amenities such as lifts and an internal communications system by means of speaking tubes".

The layout consisted of seven pavilions, each of four storeys, connected by a 200-yard corridor running the length of the site. In the 1920s it was renamed St Stephen's Hospital. After the last war the old building was gradually replaced; it has since been redeveloped as the Chelsea and Westminster Hospital, one of the most advanced medical centres in Europe, opened in 1993.

LUNATIC ASYLUMS
There were several private lunatic asylums in the neighbourhood. A Mrs Bonney ran an asylum for 'ladies suffering from milder forms of mental disease' in Old Church Street, and Alexander Cruden, compiler of a Biblical concordance, had periods when he was confined in Duffield House in Little Chelsea where the inmates were called 'pupils' and the keepers 'tutors'. A Mr and Mrs Mullins ran another asylum for ladies at Manor Cottage between Bramerton Street and Kings Road in the early 1800s.

No train to catch

A glance at the modern London Transport map confirms that there is almost an entire absence of trains in Chelsea. There is only one underground station, on its eastern border – Sloane Square. It has to be remembered that when the railway was constructed in 1868 it was built just below the surface of the road, before deep tunnel machines were available. The builders therefore encountered the difficult marshy land that stretched all the way from Pimlico, through Belgravia and Chelsea. Because of this the line goes north-west from Sloane Square to the safer ground of South Kensington and by a circuitous route eventually gets to Fulham, leaving a large area – Chelsea – unserved.

The West London line supersedes what in its day was called 'Mr Punch's railway', because its lack of success inspired a number of jokes in that journal. Officially, it was the Birmingham Bristol & Thames Junction Railway, opened in 1844 to connect a main line junction at Willesden to the basin of the short-lived Kensington Canal at Addison Road. It went, so contemporaries noted, from nowhere to nowhere and it is hardly surprising that it failed to attract customers. It closed for passenger traffic six months after it opened. Its potential was increased, however, in 1863 when it was extended along the bed of the old canal (which old waterway had utilised Counters Creek), across the Thames on the expensive Battersea Railway Bridge, and down to Clapham Junction.

Even then, it was a north-south line, without the commercial possibilities that an east-west line into London had.

By 1940 passenger traffic had ceased altogether, but in the 1990s a new initiative was taken to make use of the line, so that Willesden and Clapham Junction may be linked via Chelsea Harbour and Stamford Bridge.

Lengthy, unresolved, discussions are also still taking place on the building of a new east-west railway which would serve Chelsea.

ON THE ROADS

The absence of trains stimulated a good bus service – one of many things that Carlyle found to praise when he arrived in Chelsea in the 1830s. An omnibus then charged sixpence for the journey to the West End (a steamboat cost 2d), but this was still much cheaper than the old stage coach fares, which had been 1s 6d inside and 1s outside.

Omnibuses in London eventually had competition from trams – at first horse drawn, which could carry more than buses with less horse power. The disadvantage of trams was that the rails were a danger to other road users – horses, vehicles and pedestrians could have accidents because of them, and Chelsea Vestry was hesitant about allowing trams through its territory. When it did give approval in 1874 it was with the proviso that the route should not include Cheyne Walk, the Embankment or the Royal Hospital Road. In fact, the furthest the trams got into Chelsea was to a terminus at Beaufort Street.

104. Sloane Square station in the 1920s, with the river Westbourne running in an iron aqueduct above the line and platforms.

Town Talk

In the mid eighteenth century the population of Chelsea was about 3,000. Within a hundred years it had risen to 50,000 and by 1901 it was 75,000.

LAW AND ORDER

The nature of the countryside around Chelsea was desolate and marshy. People who travelled across the unpopulated heaths and water meadows were subject to robbery and violence. Particularly dangerous were the Five Fields, the area eventually to become Belgravia. In 1715 the Royal Hospital was asked to organise patrols of able-bodied pensioners to guard the way to London but the poor old men, despite being fitted with stout boots and thick woollen cloaks, were no match for young robbers and after one of the pensioners was killed the scheme was abandoned. Later, the Vestry took to erecting sentry boxes along the main roads and offering rewards.

Like most villages Chelsea had its medieval stocks, cage and ducking stool. These were near the church but in 1682 they were moved to the present site of Cheyne Row. For more serious offences a gibbet was erected on the border beside the Creek (the present junction of Redcliffe Gardens and Fulham Road) and it was here that three Chelsea Pensioners were hanged in chains in 1765, having been found guilty of murder.

FIRE AND DEATH

Chelsea, as a riverside village, relied heavily on watermen bringing water from the Thames to help at fires. It was Sir John Fielding who suggested that publicly available ladders would also be useful and in 1774 these were made compulsory.

For most of the nineteenth century the main Chelsea fire house was in the remains of the Petyt School in Old Church Street, but in June 1893 a handsome new station was opened in Chelsea Square. Known as 'Brompton', it nevertheless served Chelsea. It housed a steam and a manual engine, one horse cart and one fire escape with accommodation for eleven men and one coachman. In the 1930s it also had a dog which was said to stamp out fires with its paws.

The old fire station closed when the present one in Kings Road was opened in 1964.

In 1733 Sir Hans Sloane presented the parish with land to create an additional burial ground, as the churchyard was full to overflowing by then. This new ground is now laid out as a public garden, but it includes a memorial to John Martyn, a well-known botanist, who introduced peppermint and valerian into pharmacy. Such was the population increase that by 1810 more burial ground was needed, and this was taken on the east side of Sydney Street.

105. The Hans Town Association of Volunteers exercising in their Ground at Knightsbridge, 1799.

THE VOLUNTEERS

In 1799, alarmed at the prospect of a Napoleonic invasion, Chelsea, in common with many other places in the south of England, set up a body of local volunteers to resist him. Colours were presented to the 'Royal Volunteers' at a ceremony held at the Royal Hospital on 3 May 1799 by Miss North, daughter of the Bishop of Winchester. The standard had been embroidered by the ladies of Chelsea. In 1804, renamed the Chelsea Association, a body now 500 strong under the captaincy of Lord Hobart, attended a Jubilee celebration for George III at Cremorne Villa and received new colours embroidered this time by Queen Charlotte and her daughters.

Happily, the gallant band were never called upon to give service and confined their efforts to ceremonial duties such as parades from Sloane Square to Hyde Park.

LIGHTING, PAVING AND SLUMS

Whatever the inhabitants of Chelsea thought about their neighbourhood, Charles Dickens was unimpressed. Writing in *Nicholas Nickleby* in 1839 he said that "Cadogan Place was the connecting link between the aristocratic pavements of Belgravia and the barbarism of Chelsea". It was probably true that Chelsea was relatively unlit and unpaved, as shown

by an 1845 Act which permitted the Vestry powers to light streets with oil or gas, lay sewers and drains, erect urinals, provide troughs and gutters and cleanse the streets. New roads were also planned. These included the extension of Royal Hospital Road to Pimlico, and of Beaufort Street to Kensington.

In his report for 1900 Chelsea's Medical Officer noted that "We have much improved our own sewers and house drains, roads have also been widened, open spaces secured for the public and some of the worst slums of old Chelsea have been demolished. The old parish has lost much of its quaint and picturesque features but has gained immensely in health comfort and convenience."

In 1858 a new Vestry Hall was built in Kings Road to a design by W. Pocock. The duties of the new vestries of London then included the inspection and improvement of the many properties which had no running water and no sewerage. Even the Carlyles paid £1.16s a year for a single tap to the kitchen and otherwise relied on street pumps.

The first blocks of Peabody Trust buildings were erected between Cheyne Row and Lawrence Street in the 1890s, and in the north-west of the parish Lord Cadogan gave an acre of the Blacklands House garden to the Guinness Trust to build flats.

Improvements were not universally applauded. The *Daily Chronicle* in September 1909 spoke of "20,000

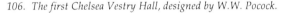

106. The first Chelsea Vestry Hall, designed by W.W. Pocock.

people being driven from Chelsea so that the members of one particular family should be enriched." The entire face of the area was being changed, the paper said, "with streets being levelled as though blown away by an enemy's guns and blocks of fashionable mansions springing up in their place." Hundreds of small traders had seen their businesses swept away and thousands of working people shipped off to all parts of London in search of homes.

In 1896 the Vestry proposed to the London County Council that the area from Battersea Bridge to Lots Road, which was a malodorous stretch of mud, should be developed, but this met with protests from residents of Cheyne Walk that the picturesque riverside scene would be destroyed. In any case, they said,

any smell there came from inadequate sewers. The scheme was not proceeded with.

LIBRARIES FOR THE MASSES

A controversial improvement was the provision of a free library. The campaign to open one was led by Benjamin Findon, and in 1887 two rooms were temporarily fitted up as reading rooms in the old Vestry Hall, which had been replaced by J.M. Brydon's Town Hall in 1886. Shortly after this the Library Commissioners were given the Manresa Road site by Lord Cadogan, plus £300 to buy technical books. The foundation stone of the building (also designed by Brydon) was laid on 8 February 1890, "a bright day with a cold north east wind", but much money to complete the library still remained to be found.

The first librarian, John Henry Quinn, was also an enthusiastic antiquarian and during his nearly forty years of service built up a collection of local history and topography as well as an Art Reference Collection. He was also the first London librarian to provide a special study room for children.

107 and 108. Posters for and against the introduction of free libraries in Chelsea in 1887. At the time the Vestry was obliged to organise a public referendum of ratepayers to approve or disapprove of the proposal. The disadvantage of this was that the people who would make most use of a free library were the very people who then did not have the right to vote.

FREE LIBRARY
FOR CHELSEA.

PUBLIC MEETING

WILL BE HELD AT THE

CHELSEA TOWN HALL,
KING'S ROAD,

In support of the adoption of the FREE LIBRARIES ACTS for CHELSEA and KENSAL NEW TOWN,

On MONDAY, MARCH 28th, 1887.

THE CHAIR WILL BE TAKEN AT 8.30 P.M., BY
THE RIGHT HON.

EARL CADOGAN.

Lord MONKSWELL,   Lord Wm. COMPTON, C.A.WHITMORE, Esq., M.P., G.A. SPOTTISWOODE, Esq., The RECTOR of CHELSEA, Rev. LAWSON FORSTER, LL.B., and other Gentlemen have promised to attend.

VOTERS OF CHELSEA.

If you do not wish the oppressive burden of your Rates increased, say NO to the Free Library Scheme.

If you do not wish to injure those Tradesmen who sell and lend Newspapers and Novels say NO to the Free Library Scheme.

If you think the Metropolis already sufficiently supplied with National Free Libraries say NO to the Free Library Scheme.

If you think Paddington, Islington, West Ham, Woolwich, Plumstead, and other great Districts of the Metropolis right when they rejected the Free Libraries this year, say NO to the Chelsea Free Library Scheme.

If you think your own Representatives upon the Chelsea Vestry right when they disapproved of a Free Library in our midst, say NO emphatically to the Free Library Scheme.

Look out for the VOTING PAPERS delivered to-day and mark them NO

A RATEPAYER.

13th May, 1887.

109. Lord Cadogan laying the foundation stone of Chelsea Library in Manresa Road on 8 February 1890. The architect, J.M. Brydon, is to the right of the man with top hat and moustache in the lower right of the picture, and Cadogan is behind him.

In September 1940 Chelsea Library was severely damaged by fire, with the loss of thousands of books, and it was not until 1951 that it was fully reopened. An even greater loss to many people was the closure of this library altogether and its transfer to part of Chelsea Town Hall, during the reorganisation of services in the new Royal Borough of Kensington and Chelsea.

110. Chelsea Library, Manresa Road. The building survives as part of the Chelsea College.

111. John Henry Quinn, Chelsea's first librarian, who began the Chelsea local history collection.

Music Makers

In 1764 an advertisement for Ranelagh Gardens included among its attractions "a performance by the celebrated and astonishing Master Mozart, a child of seven years of age who will perform several select pieces of his own composition on the harpsichord and organ". The publicity was not quite accurate – Mozart was actually eight and a half at the time. He stayed for over a year in England, seven weeks of which the family lived at a doctor's house in Five Fields Row (now Ebury Street). While he was there he wrote two symphonies, K16 and K19.

Another accomplished musician, Thomas Attwood, had not yet been born, but he was in later years to be one of Mozart's pupils. One of the founders of the Philharmonic Society and organist at St Paul's Cathedral, he spent the last years of his life at 17 Cheyne Walk.

Dr Thomas Arne (1710-1778), whose musical output is today overshadowed by his composition *Rule Britannia*, made his home for his last years at 215 Kings Road. One of his pupils, Dr Charles Burney, was appointed organist at the Royal Hospital in 1791. Burney's novelist daughter, Fanny Burney, often visited him there. It was, she said, "a sojourn so perfectly to his taste, the distance from town enough to avoid bustle, smoke, dust and noise yet not enough to impede any evening enjoyment." Dr Burney died at the Hospital in April 1814.

The artistic partnership which resulted in *Facade* took place at 2 Carlyle Square, when William Walton lodged in the attic of the Sitwell family in the 1920s. Contemporary accounts describe how Edith Sitwell (1887-1964), clad in her habitual medieval style robes, intoned the words of her poem through an instrument called the Sangerphone from behind a curtain in the front parlour to Walton's music, both of which were to become a famous ballet production.

Ralph Vaughan Williams (1872-1958) wrote many of his most famous works at 13 Cheyne Walk between 1905 and 1929, including the *Sea Symphony*, *The Lark Ascending*, the *Mass in G Minor*, *The Wasps*, the *English Hymnal* and the *London Symphony*, which features many of the street cries which could probably still have been heard on Chelsea streets. Among those who visited him there were his friends Gustav Holst and Maurice Ravel.

Sharing Vaughan Williams' interest in English folk music, Percy Grainger lived at various Chelsea addresses at about the same time (between 1902 and 1914). His first home was 26 Coulson Street, when he came to London from Australia, then 63 Oakley Street and Upper Cheyne Row and, for the longest period, at 31a Kings Road from 1908 to 1914.

112. *Wolfgang Amadeus Mozart; portrait by Pietro Lorenzoni in 1763, a year before he came to London.*

113. *An advertisement card showing Mozart with his father Leopold and his sister, published 1763/4.*

116. *Dr Charles Burney.*

114. *Dr Thomas Arne.*

117. *Béla Bartók was a frequent visitor to 18 Elm Park Gardens in the 1920s to see his friend Jelly d'Arányi, a violinist. In 1924 they gave a first performance of his First Violin Sonata at the Aeolian Hall in New Bond Street.*

115. *Thomas Attwood.*

118. Tobias Smollett, by an unknown Italian artist.

119. Leigh Hunt.

Literary Lions

TOBIAS SMOLLETT

Tobias Smollett (1721-1771) arrived in Chelsea in 1750 and there occupied half the old home of the Duchess of Monmouth in Lawrence Street, then made into two houses. The dour Scots doctor, who had served as a ship's surgeon, was already better known as a writer than for his medical skills, having produced two successful novels, *Roderick Random* and *Peregrine Pickle*. He had come to Chelsea in the hope that the healthy air might help his young daughter who was suffering from consumption.

Despite his early success, he was far from wealthy and had to devote most of his time to Grub Street journalism to pay his bills. Nevertheless, he kept a sociable household where many of his contemporaries, such as Sterne, Johnson and Garrick, would meet on Sundays to enjoy beef pudding, port and punch.

Sadly, his daughter died there in 1763, and Smollett left Chelsea. Despite its obviously unhappy memories he still described Chelsea as his second native place, and his last novel, *Humphrey Clinker*, is set partially in that neighbourhood.

LEIGH HUNT

The eccentric Leigh Hunt (1784-1859), journalist, essayist and poet, was the first of the major nineteenth century writers to choose Chelsea as his home when he came with his ragtaggle family to 22 Upper Cheyne Row in 1833. In those days the cul-de-sac contained only eight houses, all dating from the early to mid-eighteenth century, plus Cheyne House, built for the widowed Duchess of Hamilton in 1717.

Hunt was fifty and most of his life had been a hand-to-mouth existence, despite early recognition of his literary prowess, though his journalism had earned him a prison sentence for seditious libel for calling the Prince Regent "a fat Adonis".

In Chelsea he settled happily in a state of cheerful chaos in an "old fashioned house" with his once-talented wife who had taken to drink, and seven grubby, wild children. It was Hunt who was instrumental in bringing to Chelsea one of its most famous residents, Thomas Carlyle.

THE CARLYLES

Bored with life in a Dumfriesshire farmhouse, Thomas Carlyle wrote in 1834 to his brother of his intention "to look for a very modest house in the suburbs of London which we imagine may be got for £40 – Leigh Hunt talked much about a quite delightful one he

121. Jane Carlyle.

120. Thomas Carlyle, by Daniel Maclise.

has in Chelsea, all wainscotted etc., for·30 guineas".

In May Carlyle came to London and began his frustrating search, finding Kensington dirty, Brompton and Regent's Park too costly, and in the end decided that the best was that which Leigh Hunt had found him at 24 Cheyne Row.

The Carlyles arrived on 10 June 1834, having travelled from his lodgings in Clerkenwell in a Hackney cab, with Chico their canary, which burst out singing on the way, which they took to be a good omen on a damp and cloudy day. The Carlyles and the Hunts were neighbours rather than friends. Jane, Carlyle's thrifty and orderly wife was horrified by Marianne Hunt's housekeeping, described by Hunt himself as "hugger-mugger, unthrifty and sordid". But Hunt, as "cheery as a bird on a bough" spent many evenings with them. Jane played old songs on the piano and

he sang. Even at fifty he still had a "clean elastic figure" and a vestige of his dark good looks.

Mrs Hunt, on the other hand, seldom moved from her sofa, except to borrow a cup of sugar or a spoonful of tea, or even a brass fender from her neighbours. ("I had a job getting it out of her hands" wrote Jane to her mother.)

When the Hunts moved away the friendship died almost to nothing and the Carlyles settled for the rest of their lives in Cheyne Row. Jane records the domestic life of Chelsea, of Carless the butcher, Shakespeare's Dairy, Allsop the chemist, but she was adamant in getting her tea from Fortnum's. There were problems with her maids who were occasionally drunk or stupid, and slept in the kitchen.

Carlyle, on the other hand, was so much troubled by outside noise – street vendors, passing traffic and the like – that he had an attic room sound-proofed. There was, too, the problem of crowing cocks in the next door house, which Carlyle threatened to shoot. Twenty years later they were still suffering from this

122.   *The Carlyles at home in Cheyne Row; from an oil painting by Robert Tait, 1857.*

intrusion. Jane wrote that "nine large hens and a cock were sauntering under her windows from a rubbishy hen hutch erected overnight in the garden next to ours."

Carlyle also described Chelsea. The scenery, he said, was "almost opera looking" with the trees, the river and the distant view across the water and Battersea to the Surrey hills. Within a year of their arrival he had completed his history of the French Revolution, despite the. terrible setback when the manuscript was accidentally burned in John Stuart Mill's grate at Kensington Square.

The fame it brought Carlyle also brought many new visitors to the door – Ruskin, Tennyson, Dickens, Kingsley, even the flamboyant Count D'Orsay, the 'Apollo of Dandyism', who astonished neighbours by his appearance.

Jane Carlyle died in 1866, and after her death poor Carlyle, looked after by a niece, remained at Cheyne Row, silent and sad, going for lonely walks. He died in 1881.

In 1895 his house was bought by a group of admirers and eventually presented to the National Trust. It has been imaginatively furnished to allow visitors to see the kitchen where Carlyle sat smoking his pipe, and the garden where his dog Nero was buried.

JOKER WILDE

Oscar Wilde is as much Chelsea as is Carlyle and Thomas More. His connection with the area began when his widowed mother took no. 46 (later 87) Oakley Street in 1876 (the house is now gone). She was a flamboyant woman with an extravagant manner matched by an extravagant appearance, but as the years went on her son was to eclipse her literary and sartorial talents. At a time of growing fame, he married Constance Lloyd and they moved into what is now 34 Tite Street. Wilde's passion for startling decor was translated by the architect Godwin, and he changed a quite ordinary house into a stage set, which was the background for a stream of larger than life characters. In this were raised like exotic flowers the Wildes' two little boys, Vyvyan and Cyril. At the same time Wilde's reputation grew as his marvellous plays were the talk of London.

All this, as is well known, came to an abrupt end. Wilde's infatuation for Lord Alfred Douglas had far-reaching consequences. He was tried for sodomy, and given two years hard labour by the judge, who

123. Oscar Wilde, caricatured in Vanity Fair by 'Ape' in 1884.

c.1915; Dylan Thomas (1914-1953) lived and drank in Chelsea during the war at various places such as Wentworth Studios in Manresa Road, and in Markham and Godfrey Streets.

John Betjeman was a child when his family moved from Highgate to 53 Old Church Street ("the slummy end"). Much later in his life, after living in the country and having had a base in the City, he moved to 29 Radnor Walk in 1977 and remained there until his death. He fought valiantly to save the Chelsea Palace in the Kings Road. It was replaced, he said, by the cheapest and ugliest shopping and residential development in London.

Then there were the eccentric Sitwells, first at Swan Walk (1917-19) and then 2 Carlyle Square, which Osbert was to live in for the next 40 years.

BOOKS FOR CHILDREN

Wellington Square was unfashionable when A.A. Milne (1882-1956) lodged at a policeman's house (no. 8) in his young days, moving later to Embankment Gardens and then to what is now 13 Mallord Street in 1920. It was here that the famous Christopher Robin books were written. Arthur Ransome, whose books for children made him a best-seller, lived at 120 Cheyne Walk 1911-1912.

A LIFELONG BOHEMIAN

Max Beerbohm (1872-1956) lived for much of his life in Chelsea, including the important 'Bohemian' period of the 1890s. Looking back on that period, he wrote that Chelsea was fresh and a tonic.

A decade later Henry James took rooms at 10 Lawrence Street, in a house that his secretary was sharing with a friend; here he worked while he stayed at his club in London. Very soon he was captured by the atmosphere of Chelsea and took a flat at the recently-built Carlyle Mansions (no. 21) in 1913, which he described as his "Chelsea perch.... the haunt of the sage and seagull".

Another American, Mark Twain (1835-1910), came to Chelsea in 1896 when he was mourning the death of his daughter from meningitis, staying for about six months at 23 Tedworth Square. By this time he was a sad and rather embittered man as well as uncomplimentary of the art then being produced in Chelsea. He likened a painting by Turner to "a tortoiseshell cat floundering in a plate of tomatoes".

Arnold Bennett's association with the area began when he was 25 and took lodgings at 6 Netherton Grove. In his last years he lived at 75 Cadogan Square and there wrote *Riceyman Steps* and *Imperial Palace*. His almost exact contemporary and friend, John Galsworthy (1867-1933), had several London addresses, one of which was Cedar Studios in Glebe Place, described as "flimsy glass houses and brick sheds" built around the garden of the sculptor, Conrad

was his neighbour in Tite Street. While serving his sentence in Reading Gaol, his mother died.

In 1946 Sir Compton Mackenzie unveiled a plaque on 34 Tite Street commemorating Wilde's residence.

TRANSITORY POETS

John Donne (1572-1631) stayed in the Danvers household for a few years (see p.16) and may claim to be the earliest Chelsea poet. He was followed shortly afterwards by Thomas Shadwell, Poet Laureate, lawyer and playwright, who died in Chelsea in 1692, although his address is not known.

Other poets who have stayed briefly in Chelsea include Laurence Binyon (1869-1943), at 8 Tite Street in 1900; Alfred Noyes (1880-1958) at 88 Cadogan Gardens in 1924; T.S. Eliot (1885-1965) at 19 Carlyle Mansions for a few years after his arrival in England

124. *Tite Street, about ten years after Wilde's fall from society.*

Dressler. This was also much later the home of John Osborne, author of *Look Back in Anger*.

'Bram Stoker (1847-1912), author of *Dracula*, had a number of Chelsea addresses, including 27 Cheyne Walk in 1879, 18 St Leonard's Terrace (1896-1906) and 4 Durham Place in his later years.

Ian Fleming, creator of James Bond, was an occupant of Carlyle Mansions (no. 24) as was Erskine Childers (1870-1922) at no. 10, whose spy thriller *The Riddle of the Sands* was a best-seller in 1900. Somerset Maugham (1875-1965) lived at no. 27 in 1914 and he also had a residence at 213 Kings Road from 1927.

A largely forgotten novelist, Philip Gibbs (1877-1962), popular between the wars, lived in Sloane Gardens and Cadogan Gardens, and Rafael Sabatini (1875-1950), author of *Captain Blood* etc was at 22 Pont Street in the 1920s and 1930s.

P.G. Wodehouse placed his fearsome Aunt Agatha "the human snapping turtle" in Pont Street, but in real life the author (1881-1975) lived in "horrible lodgings" in Kings Road when he was working as a bank clerk and a hack writer of schoolboy stories. In more affluent days he had a home at 16 Walton Street from 1918-20. The author and playwright, Ian Hay (1876-1952), whose story of Kitchener's Army, *The First Hundred Thousand*, created a sensation in 1915, lived at 21 Cadogan Square.

125. *John Galsworthy.*

A Palette of Painters

THE BUTTERFLY SIGN
James McNeil Whistler signed his pictures with the symbol of a butterfly, formed from the initial 'W', and flitted about the Chelsea scene for nearly fifty years. He was born in America and spent much of his boyhood in Russia where his father was a major. He too was destined for an army career but found the West Point studies tedious and became a draughtsman instead. He went to Paris in 1855 and four years later he came to London. Here he stayed at 62 Sloane Street in the home of his half sister, Deborah and her husband (the latter the son of the Austen family doctor – see p.80). Whistler was next to be found in a part of Lindsey House and a few years later at 96 Cheyne Walk, the end of the terrace, where he was joined by his mother. Almost at the same time Dante Gabriel Rossetti was setting up an extraordinary household at the other end of Cheyne Walk.

Next door to Whistler was the Greaves Boatyard, whose owner had taken Turner out on the river on sunset evenings, and whose sons Walter and Henry

126. James McNeil Whistler; self portrait.

Greaves were to fall under the spell of Whistler. They too took the American artist out on the river and taught him to row with the characteristic 'Waterman's jerk'. Knowing that they were very adept at painting heraldic emblems on the sides of boats, he in turn let them watch him at work and encouraged them to try their skill on canvas and paper. Walter in particular became Whistler's most adoring student, even aping his way of dress.

In 1877 a controversial exhibition at the Grosvenor Gallery enhanced Whistler's reputation. By 1886 he had set up a "pink palace" at 454 Fulham Road near Walham Green station, but he planned something much grander, what became known as the White House at 35 Tite Street, designed by Edward Godwin. Though Whistler was fashionable he didn't impress Ruskin, who described his *Nocturne in Black and Gold* as no more than "a pot of paint flung in the public's face" and declared Whistler a coxcomb for asking 200 guineas for it.

Whistler was persuaded to sue. It was a Pyrrhic victory for although he won a protracted case, he got only a farthing damages and had to pay his own substantial legal costs. In 1879 he was declared bankrupt and he and his mistress Maud went to live in Venice, leaving the White House to be sold for £2,700, ironically to Harry Quilter, *The Times* art critic whom Whistler described as "a Philistine and parasite of art". (The White House was demolished in 1965.)

Within a year, however, Whistler and Maud were back in Chelsea at 33 Tite Street. Here his frequent visitors included Beatrix Godwin, wife of the architect, whose constant complaint was of her husband's long affair with Ellen Terry, and Walter Sickert who displaced Walter Greaves in Whistler's affections.

Maud, too, was displaced – by Beatrix Godwin – to whom Whistler became married in 1886. They settled first at no. 2 The Vale and later, in 1890, at 21 Cheyne Walk. When Beatrix died, Whistler set up a new home at 74 Cheyne Walk, built by the architect C.R. Ashbee, where he lived until his death in 1903.

THE GREAVES BROTHERS
Mystery surrounds the paintings of the Greaves brothers, many of which bear joint names. Their paintings of Chelsea, and of the river in particular, have many devotees. Despite many rebuffs Walter Greaves remained devoted to Whistler and even painted his funeral procession on its way to Chiswick churchyard. He had severe money problems and after the 1st World War was rescued by Augustus John, Sickert and Beerbohm, who gave a dinner for him at the Chelsea Arts Club; a place for him was found at the Charterhouse as a Poor Brother. He died in 1930.

127.   *Walter Greaves beside the Carlyle statue. The life-size bronze statue on Chelsea Embankment was sculpted by Joseph Boehme. It was unveiled in October 1882 by Professor Tyndall, scientist and friend of Carlyle, and a vote of thanks to Boehme was proposed by Robert Browning.*

INTO THE SUNSET

Although it is generally stated that Joseph Mallord William Turner only came to Chelsea in his old age, to a cottage at the shabby end of Cheyne Walk, it is possible that it had been his retreat for a much longer period, even while he was living at his grander address in Queen Anne Street. He was fond of disappearing to unknown retreats, and Cheyne Walk may well have been one of them.

The cottage on the site of what is now 119 Cheyne Walk was certainly his dwelling from 1847 until his death. With his ruddy complexion and rough and ready manner, Turner was known as 'The Admiral' to his neighbours and he never enlightened them as to who he was.

THE HOME OF ARTISTS

Chelsea attracted numerous artists in the nineteenth and early twentieth centuries. They included John Martin, at Lindsey Row, who specialised in vast biblical scenes with thunderous and doomladen skies. He was working on *The Last Judgement* at the time of his death in 1854.

At about the same time William Holman Hunt (1827-1910) was lodging at what is now 59 Cheyne Walk (site of Don Saltero's first coffee house – see p.75). It was here that he completed one of his most famous religious paintings, *The Light of the World.*

A leading light of the New English Art Club, Philip Wilson Steer, lived at 109 Cheyne Walk for nearly 45 years surrounded by bric-a-brac and cats. Dame Ethel Walker (1861-1951), the first woman admitted

to the New English Art Club, also lived in the company of cats. Her last exhibition, with Augustus John, was held two years before she died in 1951.

Augustus John (1878-1961) ruled Chelsea for over thirty years, first at 28 Mallord Street, where he had a house built for him by Robert van Hoff in 1914 (it was a copy of Rembrandt's studio house in Amsterdam); it was later sold to the entertainer, Gracie Fields. With his red beard, broad artist's hat and flowing cloak, he perpetuated the Bohemian era, holding court at the Café Royal. In 1935 he moved to Glebe Place and then to 33 Tite Street in 1940.

Dante Gabriel Rossetti (1828-1882) moved into 16 Cheyne Walk in 1862. It was a huge house with twelve bedrooms, a vast drawing room and an acre large garden. The rent was £110 a year, but Rossetti hoped to share this large space with other artists. The response was disappointing. His brother William came for a time, the difficult Swinburne did for a period, but Ruskin, whose way of life was too Spartan for Rossetti, was discouraged. The novelist, George Meredith was interested but soon changed his mind, not liking Rossetti's way of life.

Rossetti turned the garden into a small menagerie with inmates as varied as a white bull, two armadillos, a kangaroo and peacocks. Inside the house the furnishings were 'medieval', with plenty of blue and white china around; also kept indoors were doormice and a wombat.

Towards the end of his life Rossetti took to dosing himself with chloral and the house and garden became

128. J.M.W. Turner; watercolour by J.T. Smith.

129. Turner's House in Cheyne Walk; photograph by Hedderley.

neglected. Hall Caine moved in, hoping to bring order and security into the artist's life, but in 1881 Rossetti had a stroke and the following year died at the age of 54..

Jacob Epstein lived at 72 Cheyne Walk before the First World War and it was here that he worked on the memorial to Oscar Wilde in the Père Lachaise cemetery in Paris; his studio was bombed in 1941 when the Old Church was hit.

A contemporary artist, but far removed from Epstein in likes and dislikes, was the curmudgeonly Alfred Munnings (1878-1959), who was at 96 Chelsea Park Gardens from 1920 until his death; he was President of the Royal Academy from 1944.

John Singer Sargent (1856-1925) took a studio at what was then 33 Tite Street in 1885, followed later by his purchase of the lease of 31 (now 11) next door. He became a fashionable portrait painter and a procession of famous sitters came to the Tite Street studio; his family life, such as it was, took place at his sister's flat in Carlyle Mansions.

The extraordinary Australian artist, Mortimer Menpes (1860-1938), who became absorbed by Whistler's Japanese interest, had a large studio house built at 25 Cadogan Gardens in 1896, employing 70 Japanese craftsmen to decorate it and shipping art works from Japan in a thousand packing cases.

Captain Adrian Jones (1845-1938) was an Army veterinary surgeon, and had an extraordinary skill in sculpting horses. This is demonstrated in the splendid *Quadriga* statue which tops the arch leading to Constitution Hill, the memorial to Edward VII – this was created in the back garden of 147 Old Church Street, where he was living at the turn of the century.

William Rothenstein (1872-1945) lived in Chelsea for only a year at Glebe Place in 1900, but he was much involved in the art world there. His books give an intimate picture of life in Chelsea at the time.

Roger Fry (1866-1934), mainly responsible for promoting Post Impressionists in this country and for the establishment of the Omega Workshops, lived in Beaufort Street from 1892 to 1906.

Little is known of Walter Burgess (1845-1908), although he lived in Chelsea for over 40 years, and in that time produced some wonderful etchings of scenes at Chelsea Reach. He died in Paultons Square.

THE CHANGED SCENE

By the time of Rossetti's death the Chelsea's Thameside scene had changed drastically with the coming of the Embankment. Daniel Maclise (1806-1870) died before its construction and he described the bustle of the Cheyne Walk area – he lived at no. 4. In 1860 he listed the drawbacks of the otherwise picturesque situation – the noise of its industries, the wharfside loading, the cocks crowing, street cries and the sight of drying washing.

130. *Dante Rossetti with Hall Caine at his home in Cheyne Walk; painting by H. Treffrey Dunn, 1882.*

The Kings Road

Of all the Chelsea landmarks the Kings Road must be the most famous although, oddly, its development is comparatively recent, it having been sterilised by its reservation as a royal thoroughfare until the early years of the nineteenth century. Most likely used by Chelsea's first royal resident, Henry VIII, when visiting his mansion by the riverside (see p.14), it nevertheless remained little more than a rough field path with a rickety plank crossing the Bloody (or Blandel) Bridge at its eastern end over the Westbourne rivulet until the reign of Charles II, though a more substantial bridge existed nearer the river on the present line of Pimlico Road. In Restoration times the Kings Road was gravelled and the Bloody Bridge rebuilt in stone and although still reserved for royal use, passage and access was allowed to the inhabitants of the neighbourhood to go about their business, drive cattle and transport harvests. When in the reign of George I this privilege seemed about to be withdrawn, there was an outcry, given full support by the Lord of the manor, Sir Hans Sloane, and the Rector, Dr John King, who led a petition to the Crown for the old custom to remain. It was successful, although the road remained closed and gated to

public traffic for more than a century, with no official access except to those issued with special tokens. Possibly due to this restriction and the consequent lack of building development, the whole length of the road between Sloane Square and the Fulham boundary became renowned for its nursery gardens, although it is noticeable that the earliest of these were sited at the extreme ends of the road or else were accessible from other directions.

By 1830, when the road passed into public control, development was going on apace north and south of it. Old Church Street, Sydney Street, Manor Street, Flood Street, Beaufort and Oakley Streets were being filled up. Lord Wharton's Chelsea Park, between the Kings and Fulham Roads, was being cut into for building. First came what is now Chelsea Square and soon afterwards Camera Square (later demolished and rebuilt as Chelsea Park Gardens). The other squares, Paultons and Carlyle, on either side of the Kings Road, were to follow, but in the meaner side streets, some grim rookeries developed.

The area of The Vale was redeveloped in 1910. Previously the road had been a cul-de-sac ending at the wall of Chelsea Park paddock, and its end was marked by a 'cooling' party given by the ceramicist, William de Morgan in 1909. Other former residents included Whistler at No. 2 from 1886-1890, and Charles Shannon and Charles Ricketts, who set up

131. A 1790 view of Kings Road, identified by Alfred Beaver as 'Mrs Crouch's cottage'; drawing by him in 1890.

their Vale Press there.

Although The Vale and other enclaves like it were still pretty backwaters, William Rothenstein, one of the young bloods of the Whistler/Wilde set, had nothing good to say about the late Victorian Kings Road. "It is shabbier than Oxford Street," he wrote, "with its straggling dirty, stucco mid-century houses and shops."

Those 'straggling houses' included four which happily still survive, situated between Oakley Street and Glebe Place. These are nos. 211 to 217 and include Argyll House (211), a residence briefly (1769-70) of a Duke of Argyll, though the house was built for a John Perrin, whose monogram appears on the gate. The house was designed by the Venetian architect, Giacombe Leoni, who described it has having a "beautiful harmony of colours in brick and stone decoration - a little country house on the road to Chelsea". In later times (1922-37) it was the home of Lady Sybil Colefax, who held lavish parties there which filled the society gossip columns, in rivalry with those hosted by Mrs Syrie Maugham at no. 213 between 1928 and 1936. Nos 213 and 215 were built as a pair, the latter being the home of Dr Thomas Arne in the 1770s and in this century, the actress Ellen Terry, who came there in the 1920s towards the end of her career. No 217, on the corner of Glebe Place, was built in 1770.

All four houses were in jeopardy in the 1920s when threatened by development, but survived after public (but then unfashionable) protests were made. In the same period Box Farm was demolished to give way to a cinema. Later on, the Pheasantry could have gone the way of many fine buildings, but was saved (see p.132).

Essex House, known as 'Queen Anne's Laundry' and 'Church Place' stood on the site of Paultons Terrace until the early years of the eighteenth century, having been mentioned in 1705 as 'dilapidated and let out'. One of its occupants was Moses Goodyear, whose name appears in various documents connected with the parish in the early eighteenth century. The house, the family home in Henry Kingsley's *The Hilliers and the Burtons*, was demolished in 1840 – modern shops are now on the site.

The cottage in Glebe Place with the mansard pantiled roof, has been known as Henry VIII's hunting lodge, or the gate lodge of Shrewsbury House, and although it is one of Chelsea's older buildings it is certainly too late for those uses. The nearby 46 Glebe Place was a 'safe house' for suffragettes, and Mrs Pankhurst is said to have made an impassioned speech from one of its windows.

The Kings Parade was swept away by the building of the new fire station during the Chelsea College development in the 1970s and the future of this site

132. The cottage in Glebe Place, in the 1920s.

133. Argyll House.

is still causing concern to conservationists.

On the corner of Sydney Street, next to the burial ground, the Board of Guardians built their handsome new office in 1883: this remains. The grand town hall of J.M. Brydon might have been axed when Chelsea was merged with Kensington, but was saved. At the eastern end of the road, the Duke of York's Headquarters occupies a site previously used by the Royal Military Asylum (see p.67).

The Kings Road, essentially a local shopping area, was completely transformed from the 1960s when, rivalling Carnaby Street and Portobello Road, it became fashionable for both clothes and antiques. As the leases of grocers, dairymen, drapers and green-grocers expired they were pushed aside by coffee bars, restaurants, clothes shops, antique dealers, hair salons, and boutiques for this and that. But unlike Carnaby Street, its popularity did not diminish: on the contrary, it expanded so that today the road is a justifiable tourist attraction, its shop owners pushing out the limits of fashion and fads.

The ghosts of Whistler, Wilde and Augustus John would approve, but Carlyle would not have been amused.

MAGNIF

THE BLUE B

WORLD'S FINEST GARAGE.

A garage to accommodate 300 cars at one time and justify its claim to be the finest garage in the world will be available for motorists in London shortly after midsummer.

Any period of waiting there for the execution of repairs is to be rendered less irksome than usual by the provision of dressing rooms, a restaurant, and three lounges, one of which will be reserved for women.

This up-to-date garage is being built in King's Road, Chelsea, by the Blue Bird Motor Co., Ltd., which yesterday celebrated the first anniversary of its petrol service by lowering the price of No. 1 spirit from 1s. 5d. to 1s. 4d. a gallon.

A feature of the new building is that there will be no pillars to restrict freedom of movement. The top floor, with an unobstructed area of 18,000 square feet, will be the biggest room of its kind in London.
—*Daily Sketch.*

. . . When the scheme is complete in every detail London will possess a garage that in size alone will probably rank as one of the largest public motor garages in the world. This new pioneer structure is so original in its conception, so unique in general lay-out and the service it will render to the motorist, that it seems almost like a garage transformed bodily from the Utopia of the novelist's imagination. The site for this wonder garage has been admirably chosen, fronting as it does on the King's Road and nearly an acre in extent. Fifteen cars can replenish with oil and petrol at the same time. When the "Colossus" of motor garages itself is completed it will contain, among other things, extensive modern repair shops, new car show-rooms, a large motor-cycle depot, and lounges and club-rooms for the use of the company's clients, &c. Completeness is the keynote of the building.
—*Financial News.*

The now famous Blue Bird Hire Service is to be strengthened and soon there will be put into service a number of Rolls-Royce cars, which it is claimed will make the Blue Bird Service streets ahead of any other, and at no higher charge than that in existence.

The heavy demand at present for garage accommo-dation and service has induced the company to start on a scheme which involves an outlay of over £60,000, and which will provide London with one of the finest garages in the world. It will be a three-floored building in which runways of easy gradient will connect each floor. The latest mechanical devices will be installed. A feature of the proposed structure is that the upper floors will be suspended from the roof instead of being supported from the floor. This will provide a huge ground floor space free of any obstruction in the shape of supports, and will be a unique feature in garage construction.

A steel turntable will be provided at every entrance, so that no matter how crowded the floor space may be cars will be easily backed into a small corner. Lounges and other up-to-date conveniences will be provided for motorists, and it is hoped that the garage will be avail-able for use about four months hence.

The success hitherto attained by the Blue Bird Com-pany bids fair to be extended, and is proof positive of an oft-repeated assertion that healthy competition forms an excellent stimulus to industry.
—*The Morning Advertiser.*

330—3

PETROL SERVICE

THE P

134. Advertisement for the Blue Bird garage, 330-340 Kings Road, which claimed to be the largest petrol station in the country. It offered '60 tyre inflation points' and lounges and clubrooms. The building is currently being refurbished.

...h are not converted & inaccessible stables "Daily Express"

VIEW OF THE NEW

...NT MODERN GARAGE

...URSE OF CONSTRUCTION BY

... MOTOR COMPANY, LIMITED

OPEN DAY AND NIGHT

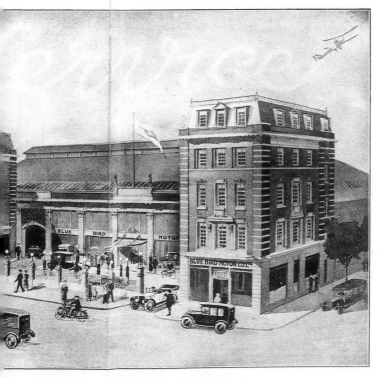

Some Outstanding Features

SITE COVERS 23,500 SUPER FEET.

GARAGE FLOOR AREA, 50,000 SUPER FEET.

THREE FRONTAGES.

PARKING SPACE FOR 300 CARS.

WORKSHOPS COVER 7,000 SUPER FEET.

60 TYRE INFLATION POINTS.

LOUNGES & CLUBROOMS FOR LADIES ONLY, OWNER-DRIVERS, VISITING CHAUFFEURS.

READING & WRITING ROOMS.

ROLLS-ROYCE & DAIMLER SERVICES.

...ON THEIR EXTENSIVE SITE

...NG'S ROAD, CHELSEA, S.W.3

AT THE REAR OF THEIR

...ION—THE LARGEST IN THE COUNTRY

...SENCE OF TARIFFS DOES NOT AFFECT THIS COMPANY'S BUSINESS

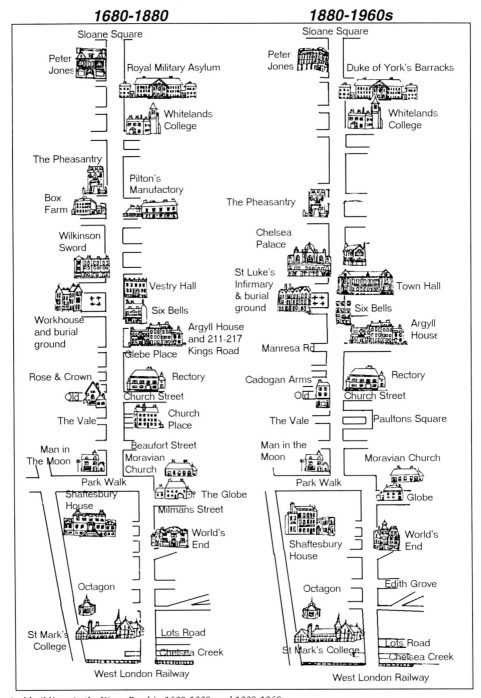

135. *Principal buildings in the Kings Road in 1680-1880, and 1880-1960s.*

Left hand map: *Peter Jones 1877, rebt 1880; The Pheasantry c.1820-; Box Farm c1680-1900; Wilkinson Sword 1870-1902; Workhouse 1737, rebt 1870; burial ground 1736; Rose &Crown c1719; Shaftesbury House 1689-1856; St Mark's College 1840-1970s; Royal Military Asylum 1801-1909; Whitelands College 1842-1930s; Pilton Manufactory 1809; Six Bells c.1780, rebt 1900; 211-217 Kings Road 1750; Church Place c1640-1840; Moravian Church 1753; World's End c.1670, rebt c.1850.*
Right hand map: *Peter Jones rebt 1936; The Pheasantry c.1820; Chelsea Palace 1902-1960s; Shaftesbury House (Workhouse Infirmary, St Stephen's) 1856-1980s; Duke of York's Barracks 1909-; Whitelands College rebt 1890; dem. 1930s; Town Hall 1886; Six Bells 1870-; Cadogan Arms 1890s; World's End c.1910*

Little Chelsea

The term 'Little Chelsea' was used by John Rocque on his map of the 1740s to describe the western part of the parish lying between the Fulham boundary and the World's End, before the curious kink in the Kings Road known still as 'Moravian corner' – this feature was probably caused by land ownership, as it follows the wall of Lord Wharton's Chelsea Park and the edge of the Beaufort House grounds.

Although somewhat remote from the riverside village of Chelsea, Little Chelsea was considered quite a desirable neighbourhood and by the mid seventeenth century several important houses had been built there, although some residents, such as Lord Verney, later Lord Fermanagh, living with his wife at his father's house there in the 1690s, found his journeys to the City a tedious business. By road it was unsafe "because of rogues" and by river, cold, apart from the long walk in dirt and dark, if not rain.

Their home, once known as Brickhills, and later as Stanley or Grove House, stood in spacious gardens not far from the Creek and its crossing by Stanley or Stone bridge.

Although early maps give few details, Verney had several important neighbours, among them the 3rd Earl of Shaftesbury, Anthony Ashley Cooper, who had been driven out of London by the effect of its 'great smoak' on his asthma. His Shaftesbury House, on the more northerly Fulham Road, was later to become the home of the antiquarian Narcissus Luttrell, and was eventually absorbed into the workhouse and St Stephen's Hospital.

Stanley House was taken in 1777 by the botanist and horticulturalist, the Countess of Strathmore, an ancestor of the Queen Mother. Subsequent inhabitants included William Hamilton, the British Envoy at the court of Naples and an antiquarian, who was among those responsible for bringing the Elgin marbles to Britain.

By the 1820s the Chelsea Creek had become a canal and Dudmaston House, another villa beside it, was joined by a timber mill and a brewery, although still surrounded by nursery gardens. Grazing rights on four acres of Lammas Lands there prevented building around the eighteenth-century Ashburnham House, which in its prime had been a residence to rival any in the district. It was "built in antique style" for Dr Benjamin Hoadley, son of the Bishop Hoadley Subsequent residents included Lady Mary Coke, known by London society as 'the White Cat', who had moved there from Aubrey House in Kensington, and finally the Earl of Ashburnham before the house was sold in 1862 as a pleasure garden.

Among the events in its short life in this guise were public trips in a captive balloon, which was filled at the nearby gas works (the Balloon public house in Kings Road was named for it). Within ten years or so all this went so that Alfred Beaver could write in 1892 that "The Creek is now a dirty ditch lined with ugly wharves and sheds, railway engines dashing past constantly and a wilderness of more or less dingy streets covers the farmlands and gardens."

These 'dingy streets' have now been cleared away in modern developments, some of them very ugly, but with facilities such as shops, doctors' surgeries and even a theatre, which are doubtless an improvement on the wretched multi-occupied streets of the past, for all their fabled neighbourliness.

137. Chelsea Creek and Stanley Bridge; drawing by Walter Greaves.

136. Shaftesbury House.

138. Cheyne Walk, by John Varley.

The Lost Town

The heart of Chelsea up to the end of the eighteenth century was around the Old Church, near the riverside. The bustle and influence in the parish then began to move north and east, and the building of St Luke's in Sydney Street in 1824, and the release of Kings Road to public property in 1830, confirmed the shift. The construction of the Chelsea Embankment in the early 1870s swept away vestiges of now forgotten streets, wharves and boatyards, making redundant the shops, pubs and businesses which served them. The Embankment altered the intimate relationships which existed between Chelsea and the river – buildings which previously had gardens sloping down to the water, were now forcibly detached from it.

However, the work of the photographer Hedderley (see p.121) and the Greaves brothers perpetuate the names of some of the traders in the 1860s and 1870s, such as Spell's post office and general store, Morrison's the artists' colourman, Morgan's dairy, and Stevens the baker.

Before the Embankment, Cheyne Walk ran only from no. 1 to no. 27 (nos. 7 to 13 were rebuilt in the 1880s) and as the old names and terraces disappeared and building increased the numbering was extending, often with confusing results.

Duke Street was the continuation of Lombard Street beyond the junction with Danvers Street. At the end of Duke Street the river was in view with the approach to Battersea Bridge, and on the corner could be seen the elegant Belle Vue House and Belle Vue Lodge (nos 91 and 92 Cheyne Walk) built on land sold by the Moravians. These houses survived construction, as did Lindsey Row, the divided Lindsey House where at no. 4, now 98 Cheyne Walk, Isambard Kingdom Brunel spent his young days from 1808 to 1824. He designed the Clifton Suspension Bridge and the *Great Eastern* steamship. Brunel's father, Mark, is blamed for some unacceptable alterations to the old house, later remedied at great cost.

Some forty years later, Whistler came to live first at 101 and then at 96, where his neighbours were the famous Greaves boatmen (see p.97).

Although the local effects of the Embankment were mainly destructive, the exception was the eastern end

139.   The riverside at Chelsea, a photograph by James Hedderley c.1870, from the tower of Chelsea Old Church.

140.   Cheyne Walk c.1868, also by Hedderley.   Looking east from the Kings Head and Eight Bells.

141. *Lombard Street and Arch House.*

142. *The north side of Duke Street near the river, in 1873. Demolition of the south side of the street is taking place.*

143. Chelsea waterfront before the Embankment; oil painting by Ernest Robinson, exhibited in 1890.

of Cheyne Walk, where as the new river wall was completed the Board of Works released some land surplus to its requirements for building. These were snapped up by the well-to-do, who commissioned fashionable architects such as Norman Shaw to build new houses which became the row known as Chelsea Embankment, divided by the Physic Garden. The houses included Turner's Reach House, Cheyne House and the Clockhouse, all by Shaw, plus others by Edward Godwin and George Bodley, and what has been described as "a Victorian country house brought to town", by Phené Spiers, built for the judge, Sir Robert Collier.

Cheyne Walk was now separated from the river by the Embankment and the Embankment Gardens. The old pub, the King's Head and Eight Bells on the corner with Cheyne Row was to last into the next century, but the small shops that then existed, the Cricketers inn and the Thames Coffee House on the corner of Lawrence Street, were soon to be demolished for the erection of Carlyle Mansions in the

1880s. Lombard Terrace, which survived into the 1890s, contained Maunder's Fish Shop, patronised by Jane Carlyle. This was to be replaced by an art nouveau house by C.R. Ashbee, as 74 Cheyne Walk, built for Whistler. By the 1930s only four old buildings remained on this terrace and when their demise was signalled, the Chelsea Society mounted a campaign to save them, but to no avail. The tenant of a toy shop on the corner of Old Church Street barricaded herself in as workmen arrived to demolish. With her shop went the Lombard Café, frequented by Orpen, John and Steer, who used to sit out under its awning. Much of the redevelopment was, in fact, lost to bombing in April 1941.

Before the Embankment was built the riverside between the Old Church and Battersea Bridge was hidden behind the buildings of Lombard Street and Duke Street, and was reached through the Arch House. This curious building spanned the entrance to Lombard Street and although at the time of its demolition it bore the mundane legend of 'Alldin s

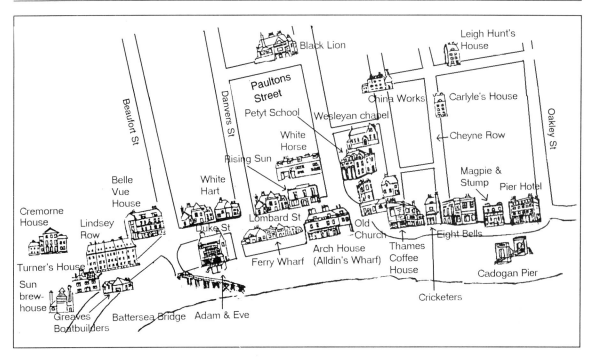

144. The Old Town c.1869 before the construction of the Embankment. Cremorne House c.1780; Sun brewhouse c.1830; Battersea Bridge 1771-1887; Lindsey Row c.1675; Belle Vue House 1771; Petyt School 1705; Black Lion c.1690; Eight Bells 1771; Pier Hotel 1844-1968; Cadogan Pier 1841.

145. After the construction of the Embankment 1874: Lots Rd Power Station 1904; Battersea Bridge 1890; Crosby Hall 1910; Ashbee House (72 Cheyne Walk) 1888-1941; Holy Redeemer Church 1895; Cheyne Hospital 1898; Dr Phené's House 1901-1920

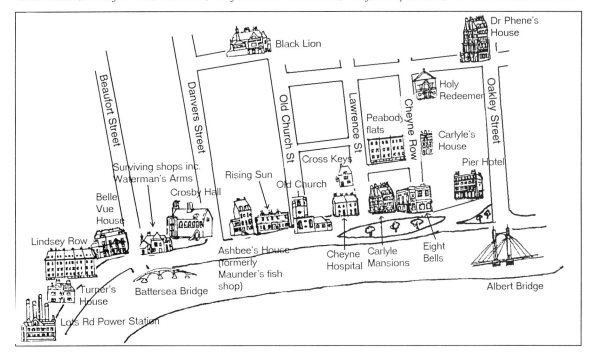

146. Paradise Row, from a watercolour by G. Munson.

Coal Wharf', it had, according to popular folk lore, been the home, or site of the home, of the sixteenth-century Bishop of London, Richard Fletcher and his son, the dramatist John Fletcher. It is shown in many of the works of Walter Greaves.

Oddly, after all these losses, a very old building was inserted into the Chelsea landscape near the Embankment. This was Crosby Hall, built in Bishopsgate 1466-75, for the City magnate, Sir John Crosby. The truncated remains of the house (aptly, once owned by Sir Thomas More) were moved from the City between the wars and re-erected under the auspices of the University and City Association of London to the corner of Danvers Street (part of More's garden) where, in 1926-7, it was incorporated into a Tudorish building, designed by W. Godfrey for the British Federation of University Women. Unfortunately, the abolition of the Greater London Council, which owned the building, has meant that the Hall has been sold to a private purchaser and is no longer open to the public.

PARADISE LOST

Further east from Danvers Street was Paradise Row. This was an old part of Chelsea which was lost after the construction of the Embankment, when the Royal Hospital Road was built to its present size to link the Embankment and Sloane Street in c.1906. By then, many of the buildings in it were slums, but it was certainly picturesque. It was by then essentially a working-class road, full of laundries and jobbing builders, and it excited little public sympathy. Despite the efforts of Chelsea historian, Reginald Blunt, it was taken down in the name of progress.

CHELSEA HARBOUR

In 1892 the historian Alfred Beaver mourned the passing of the old rural suburbs. "The great houses which gave Chelsea its fame have all but disappeared and the quaint old streets, or 'rows,' as so many of them were called, will soon have disappeared too. Where is the Westbourne – a wood skirted trout-stream of olden days or even the little rivulet on the western boundary? One is now a sewer, a railroad occupies the site of the other. Gone, too, is the belt of open land which fringed the little village – the Lots, the Lammas Lands...."

The Lots had certainly gone and around Chelsea Creek there were coal yards and docks, Viger's timber yard, refuse dumps and other unlovely occu-

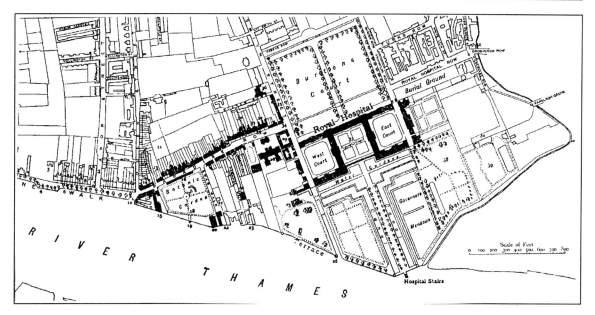

147. *Map showing the old route of Paradise Row, now obliterated by the continuation of Royal Hospital Road down to the Embankment.*

pants. Poor Beaver might have been somewhat cheered had he been able to look ahead a century.

"I dreamed of a great scheme on the bank of the Thames," said the architect, Ray Moxley, of Chelsea Harbour. In the 1980s, twenty acres of this industrial wasteland were bought by P&O and Globe to produce what they described as a "unique world of houses, flats, offices, restaurants and shops and a luxury hotel built around a working yacht harbour." There is a vast underground car park and the central Belvedere Tower is topped by a tidal ball which gauges the height of the tide. The architecture is a mixture of classical and modernistic, much in the mood of Docklands, and although the prices are high the development is not exclusive – the general public can enjoy many of its amenities and the riverside walk.

But what might be considered a prestigious improvement to this once down and out corner of Fulham (for like Chelsea Football Club, Chelsea Harbour is outside Chelsea) received a chilly welcome from Fulham's local authority which proposed to the Boundary Commission that Chelsea Harbour should be transferred to Kensington and Chelsea. But the offer aroused no enthusiasm on the other side of the boundary, both councils taking the view that the Harbour would be a liability. The Harbour, therefore, remains in Fulham.

148. *The Chelsea Harbour development, a small town built on derelict land.*

149. Lots Road Power Station in the 1920s.

Power Structure

There is irony in the fact that the source of power for much of London's vast underground railway system is situated in Chelsea – an area almost entirely devoid of stations.

Lots Road Power Station rises in solid industrial majesty, unmoved among the new developments of Chelsea riverside, keeping the wheels turning, its remaining two chimney stacks plumed with white vapour, while the rest of London's old power stations lie defunct and derelict. Generally condemned as hideous monstrosities in their early days, these industrial cathedrals, together with railway termini, have acquired a romantic status at this end of the century.

The earliest parts of the underground system – what are now the Circle and inner London District and Metropolitan lines – used steam engines. Then, in 1890, the world's first electrically operated 'tube' railway, the City and South London Railway was opened. The success of this, and the potential of electric trains using deep level tunnels then made possible by engineering advances, led to the swift creation of what is now the basis of the present inner system – the Central Line (1900), Bakerloo Line (1906), Piccadilly Line (1906) and Northern Line (1907).

While all these new London facilities were being built a monopoly of them was gradually acquired by an American, Charles Yerkes, whose aim, when he floated the Underground Electric Railways Company of London in 1902, was to acquire the Metropolitan and District lines, to finance the construction of the Bakerloo, Piccadilly and Northern lines, and to build a vast power station at Lots Road to fuel them. The site of Lots Road had the advantage of being able to receive coal from the river.

There was much local opposition, which included Whistler, to the power station scheme. The magazine *Punch*, when it saw the plan for four chimney stacks, suggested that a large statue of Carlyle should be mounted on top of them.

Despite it being an obvious wartime target, the station survived the war despite many incidents. In 1963 there was a major overhaul when it was converted from coal driven to oil driven; two of its chimneys were demolished as they were no longer necessary. Today the Underground relies on Lots Road and another generating station at Greenwich for two thirds of its needs – the latter being a peak-load and supplementary facility, the rest coming from the National Grid.

150. Henry Holland's 'Pavilion' in Hans Town; engraving published in 1810.

Sloanes and Slums

HANS TOWN

Henry Holland, architect to the Georgian aristocracy, began developing Sloane Street and adjacent roads in 1777 on 89 acres of land leased from the Cadogan family. At the time there was open terrain – the Five Fields – towards London, and the Westbourne river still flowed through the marshy land – the stream now crosses Sloane Square station above the platforms in a pipe (*see* ill. 104). By 1790 the so-called Hans Town (after Hans Sloane) consisted of handsome houses on the west side of Sloane Street and turnings off it – Hans Place, Street and Crescent. On the east, the grander Cadogan Place facing its own private gardens, was a later development.

To the south of Hans Place Henry Holland reserved a number of acres for himself. Here he built a house called Sloane Place, nicknamed The Pavilion, in recognition of his creation of the Prince Regent's first fanciful pavilion at Brighton. Holland's own edition was a comparatively modest affair, only two storeys high, with pillars supporting a rear canopy, but its main beauty was in its elegant internal decorations and its spacious grounds, laid out by Holland's father-in-law, Lancelot 'Capability' Brown; these included grottos, a 'ruined castle', an ornamental bridge over a lake and an ice house made up as a folly.

Sloane Street, connecting Knightsbridge and the newly-formed Sloane Square, was mainly one of genteel trade – hairdressers, milliners, dressmakers, fan makers and the like – but though the building of the street proceeded quickly enough the land either side was still mostly empty in the Regency period. A paddock is shown on a map of that period extending all the way from Hans Place to Sloane Square, backing on to the houses of Sloane Street. But such was the prestige of the development, especially to the east where it joined up with Belgravia, that even the Cadogans abandoned their home south of the Kings Road (the site was taken by the Royal Military Asylum) and built a new mansion between Lowndes Street and Sloane Street, in modern years displaced by a large hotel.

The very popularity of Hans Town was its undoing. There were too few houses in too much space and when by 1851 the Great Exhibition had helped to put this area on the map, and Cubitt had succeeded in draining the Five Fields to build Belgravia, the temptation for developers was too great. Soon, Henry Holland's Georgian villas were replaced with what Osbert Sitwell called 'Pont Street Dutch', and red bricked houses and mansion flats crowded behind the Sloane Street frontage. Cadogan Square and Lennox Gardens took up the gardens that 'Capability' Brown had landscaped and only the name Pavilion Road reminds us of a more spacious era.

151. Premises at the top end of Sloane Street early this century.

CHELSEA COMMON

When Sloane Street was first built there was still countryside to the west, firstly around Blacklands, a former home of the Marquis of Winchester, which was then a lunatic asylum, and then came Chelsea Common, an area bounded today by Fulham Road, Sydney Street, Kings Road and Draycott Avenue. This was a piece of land on which many residents had grazing rights, with one section reserved for the poor. (An inn called the Cow and Two Calves is marked on an early map near the cattle pound on the northern boundary, and there was also a pond formed by gravel digging: Pond Place is a reminder of this.)

In 1790 the Cadogans obtained an Act of Parliament to secure the Common's enclosure and to allow building leases. Alfred Beaver, a hundred years later, wrote that the site of the Common was "a labyrinth of streets, mainly narrow and squalid". Nor was this poor area limited to the old Common boundaries. It was replicated in the vicinity of the Royal Hospital, and Paradise Row was deteriorating into a cluster of alleys and courts, with lodgings used by thieves and prostitutes.

Similarly, the districts around Lower Sloane Street and Sloane Gardens had become shabby thoroughfares of third-class housing and shops in the latter half of Victoria's reign. Turks Row and Jews Row,

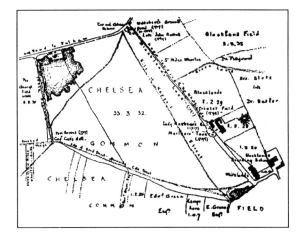

152. Map of Chelsea Common, 1769.

once the site of the old Bun House at the end of Pimlico Road (the former named for a coffee house which stood there) had now sunk into seriously Dickensian squalor, so none mourned their passing when they were replaced by new streets and the modern blocks of Sloane Court.

Chelsea Barracks on the Westminster side of Chelsea Bridge Road were opened in 1862 to accommodate

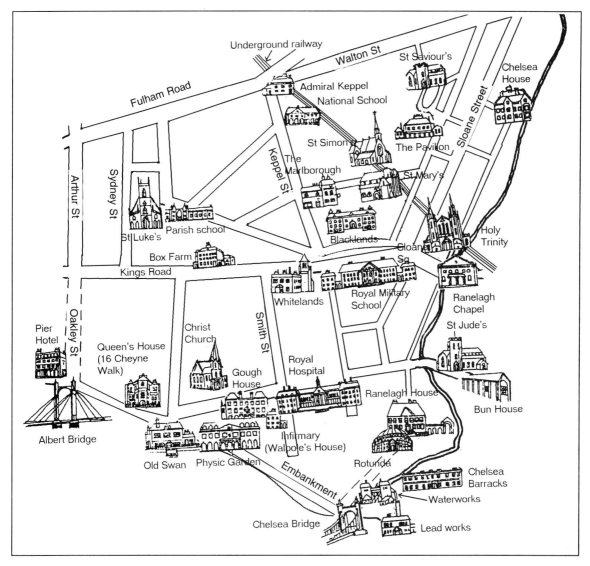

153. Eastern Chelsea builds up 1800 –. Pier Hotel 1844; Albert Bridge 1873; Old Swan dem. 1876; Christ Church 1839; Infirmary 1816; Admiral Keppel rebt 1856; National School c.1830; Blacklands dem. 1890; Royal Military School 1803; St Simon Zelotes1859; St Saviour's 1840; Chelsea House (Lord Cadogan's) 1874; The Pavilion 1777-1879; St Mary's, Cadogan Street1882; Holy Trinity, Sloane Street 1828; Ranelagh Chapel 1819-43; St Jude's 1855; Ranelagh House dem. 1805; Rotunda dem. c.1806; Bun House closed 1839; Chelsea Barracks 1860; Waterworks closed 1892; Lead works c.1800; Chelsea Bridge 1858

a thousand men (the foundations were laid on the anniversary of the Battle of Inkerman). Changes in boundaries in 1899 were to result in the barracks being placed outside Chelsea. The original buildings were replaced by modern barracks in 1960.

CLEARING SLUMS

Another poor area, south west of Cadogan Square, served the wealthy of that square and Hans Town.

Here lived brickmakers, builders, butchers, bakers, chimney sweeps, coal men, dustmen, street sweepers and night soil men in a slum area that at its best was represented by Marlborough Road, in which street Peter Jones first set up shop. At the end of the nineteenth century the authorities began to clear the area of slums, but the rejoicing was drowned by the protests of those being cleared. The *Daily Chronicle* in 1909 told of 20,000 people being driven out and of artisans' dwellings being levelled and small trad-

154. Demolition in Sloane Square 1892.

ers' businesses swept away, as the new Sloane Avenue and Draycott Avenue obliterated what had been there before. Though these roads were laid out they were not entirely occupied. A few large houses were built and blocks of flats such as Cadogan Court were erected, but for over twenty years much of this miserable district remained in limbo until the 1930s when, despite violent local opposition – an Eviction Defence Army, 300-strong, fought off the developers with sticks, bells and whistles – Sloane Avenue Mansions, Nell Gwynne House and Cranmer Court appeared.

Also built were the ten-storey blocks of Chelsea Cloisters, which occupied almost the whole island site between Sloane Avenue, Ixworth Street and Makin and Elystan Streets. This controversial development generated protests for over a decade in postwar years. Nearby in Rawlings Street a large site, vacant for years, was filled with two hundred local authority flats after the last war.

Sloane Square, with its houses-turned-shops, was also transformed. A photograph of *c.*1864 shows that the corner where the Peter Jones department store later stood, was occupied by the Star and Garter, a shoe shop and a pawnbrokers. A photograph of about 1892 (above) shows modest shops about to be demolished. They include that of Sir Thomas Dodd, who sold glass shades and offered 'No Tick', next to Shields Printing Works, reduced to Lot 59. Berzolla's, a confectioner's next to the station, a local landmark, remained in business until 1938, but in Sloane Street, Mme Leah Nathalie, who had opened her fan shop in the 1880s when fans were a fashion accessory, closed it in 1912 when they were not.

Certainly until the end of the nineteenth century Sloane Square was not a self-contained haven – Kings Road went diagonally across it towards Eaton Square, and Sloane Street carried south across it to join Lower Sloane Street.

The First World War memorial was moved amid some controversy in the 1930s. In 1958 a nude figure fountain by Gilbert Ledward was installed at the west end of the Square as a gift from the Royal Academy.

Pens and Lens

THE HISTORIANS

Chelsea history owes much to early historians such as John Bowack and Thomas Faulkner, to John King, Alfred Beaver, Reginald Blunt and William Gaunt. Later commentators on Chelsea have included Thea Holme, Tom Pocock and Michael Bryan, whose exhibitions at the Alpine Gallery in the 1980s were histories in themselves.

Bowack, an industrious historian, without whose efforts much of the history of west London would not have survived, lived in Old Church Street in 1705 at the time his first volume of *The antiquities of Middlesex* (including Chelsea) appeared. In his Chelsea the first pensioners were settling in at the Royal Hospital and Don Saltero's coffee house was flourishing. Sadly, his work never got beyond the first volume. It is, to modern minds, tediously detailed, but then, if he had been more of an editor much of the information of that period would have been pencilled out.

His neighbour in Church Street was the Rector of Chelsea, Dr John King, a livelier but equally zealous antiquarian, who wrote of people as well as of places.

Histories of west London areas would be sketchy indeed without the labours of Thomas Faulkner. Most of his work was done when he was living in Chelsea, where he kept a bookshop and print shop on the corner of Paradise Row, the later site of the

155. Thomas Faulkner; painting by Thomas Clater.

Chelsea Pensioners pub. Born in 1777, his first published material appeared in the *Gentleman's Magazine*, a periodical to which he contributed for over fifty years. In 1810 he produced his *History of Chelsea*, followed by the *History of Kensington* (1820), and two volumes of a new history of Chelsea in 1829.

After Paradise Row he moved to 27 Smith Street and advertised as the Cadogan Library: "an extensive and valuable collection of works in history, divinity, topography, antiquities, voyages and travels, lives and memoirs, poetry and drama". His book on Chelsea was first published in 17 monthly parts at 2s 6d each, before being bound into two volumes.

However, Alfred Beaver in 1892, while paying tribute to Faulkner's conscientious approach, accuses him of "astonishing errors" in recording details such as the epitaphs in the Old Church, and "committing the grave fault, common to many topographical writers of his day, of taking everything upon trust."

THE PHOTOGRAPHERS

As well as historians, Chelsea has also been blessed with photographers. They include James Hedderley, succeeded in our own times by John Bignell. All that is known about Hedderley is that he was born in 1815, and spent some years from 1860 taking photographs of Chelsea. He used a 10" x 12" view camera and tripod and used long time exposures. We can, through his pictures, walk in a vanished Duke or Lombard Street, where a baker's boy stands and gazes across Cheyne Walk, catch the horse bus at Sloane Street, or loiter with others to watch navvies digging the Embankment, or catch a final glimpse of old shops before their shutters went down for the last time.

John Bignell has walked through Chelsea with more modern equipment, but the same feeling for the ephemeral and its worth is in his work.

THE CHELSEA NEWS

The history of the local newspaper, the *Chelsea News*, is made confusing by frequent changes of name. It does seem certain, however, that its roots go back to 1860 with the appearance of the *West London Times*, which then changed to the *Chelsea News* in 1865. In the 1890s, dissatisfied with the "strictly impartial view the *Westminster and Chelsea News* and the *West London Press* took in political matters", Unionists subscribed £2,000 to buy the *West Middlesex Advertiser* to propound their views. In 1939 the *Chelsea News* swallowed this rival and for the rest of its independent life continued to play an important role in Chelsea life under its editor, Jim Barnard and Chief Reporter, Bill Raymond.

In the 1970s the *Chelsea News*, together with nine other newspapers in west London, was bought out by the London Newspaper Group.

Playbill

THE ROYAL COURT

Despite Chelsea's strong association with the arts, its theatrical history is restricted, though illustrious. The earliest mention of a public playhouse was the brief existence of a theatre in the stable of Lord Wharton's house in Church Lane in 1705, when a letter from his uncle to Lord Fermanagh speaks of "a fine scaramouche" (clownish comedy) being performed there by the Duke of Southampton's servants. Otherwise there was the occasional dramatic performance at Ranelagh Gardens.

In 1870, what had previously been a dissenters' chapel in what is now Sloane Gardens was opened as the New Chelsea Theatre. Tantalisingly, Horwood's map of London in the early part of the nineteenth century shows this site occupied by a theatre, but nothing is known about it. The intention of the New Chelsea was to capitalise on the fact that the inhabitants of this growing part of town had no playhouse nearer than the Haymarket. But the usual fare of comedies and light dramas was not a success, despite an elaborate conversion of the interior, until 1885 when a highly popular series of Pinero farces was begun. Rebuilding on this side of Sloane Square in 1887 forced the theatre, by then called the Court or Royal Court, to close.

It was reopened in a new building next to the Underground station, designed by Walter Emden and W.R. Crewe, on 24 September 1888. It was generally successful, even attracting the Prince of Wales and the Duke of York to a Pinero revival. In 1904 a very successful artistic management by Granville Barker and J.E. Vedrenne began, which featured plays by new writers such as Shaw and Galsworthy in a series of well patronised short runs.

156. The interior of the Ranelagh Chapel, before conversion to the Court Theatre.

After the First World War the concentration on new plays continued – first productions of Shaw's *Heartbreak House* and *Back to Methuselah* included – but by the 1930s, in common with other theatres, the Royal Court was struggling against the competition of cinema. The last success was an extraordinarily long run of Eden Phillpotts' *The Farmer's Wife*, which ran from 1924 to 1927.

The building was used as a cinema from 1935 until 1940, when the bomb which caused so much havoc at Sloane Square station also wrecked the theatre, which did not re-open until 2 July 1952, this time under the aegis of the London Theatre Guild. Early successes included *Airs on a Shoestring* (1954) and *The Threepenny Opera* (1956). It was in 1956 that the theatre was taken over by George Devine and his English Stage Company. A new and famous era began, for it was under Devine's management that John Osborne's *Look Back in Anger* and *The Entertainer* were produced, as well as a trilogy of plays by Arnold Wesker, and others by Harold Pinter and Samuel Beckett. In this period of artistic resurgence, the tiny Theatre Upstairs opened in November 1971.

The Royal Court remains one of the brightest theatrical stars in the London firmament, but it has always struggled financially. In 1994 its young

157. Programme for the first production of Shaw's Heartbreak House at the Royal Court in 1921.

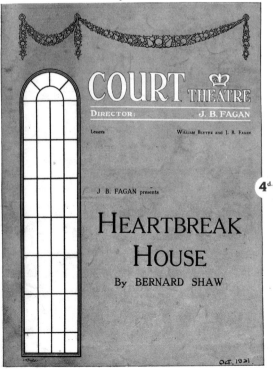

158. The interior of the new Royal Court Theatre, February 1871.

director, Stephen Daldry, reported on the physical decay of the building. "The drains flood the understage and the stalls in winter just as they did in Shaw's day and the admin offices are a Dickensian rabbit warren, the stage machinery hopelessly inefficient and the front of house facilities awful." He was hoping then for a Lottery grant and two weeks later got one. This year (1996) the Royal Court will close for two years for work to be done, but its productions will continue at the Duke of York's and those of the Theatre Upstairs will be presented at the Ambassador's.

THE CHELSEA PALACE

The only other theatre in Chelsea of any size was the Chelsea Palace, a music hall built in 1903 at 232-242 Kings Road to the designs of Wylson and Lang. It accommodated over 2,500 people.

In its heyday the Palace attracted all the famous names such as Robey, Tilley, Georgie Wood and Gracie Fields, and its Christmas pantomimes were the highlight of the year for several generations of local children. Even after the last war, Clarkson Rose's musical shows such as *Twinkle*, and Paul Raymond's mixture of circus and nude shows were still filling the stalls. The Palace closed (apart from one season) in 1957, whereupon it was bought by Granada to use as a television studio, finally being demolished in the 1960s.

159. *The Chelsea Palace early this century.*

ON THE FRINGE

Oddly, Chelsea was scarcely affected by the boom in pub theatres in the 1960s, but in 1982 the Man in the Moon Theatre was opened in a converted cold storage area behind the pub of the same name in Kings Road. This has produced plays of a wide range in the last fourteen years, the aim being to allow artistes maximum freedom in their work. The theatre has over sixty seats and runs for 48 weeks a year. In its comparatively short life the Man in the Moon has had a number of successes and has greatly contributed to Chelsea's artistic reputation.

In 1992 the Chelsea Theatre Centre in the World's End development was launched under the artistic direction of Francis Alexander. Committed to the presentation of new adaptations of rarely-performed European classic plays, it opened with Feydeau's *Monsieur Chasse*.

THEATRE PEOPLE

Despite the dearth of local theatres, a number of famous thespians have chosen Chelsea to live in. At 57 Pont Street was Sir George Alexander (1858-1918), an actor-manager, who took over the St James's Theatre in 1891 and there presented brilliant seasons of plays by Wilde, Pinero and Sutro. Two of Wilde's

plays were in the West End at the time of his trial and conviction in 1895 and such was the hypocrisy of the time that his name was blanked out on the billboards, though the plays were not taken off. Alexander bought the acting rights of the plays and bequeathed them to Wilde's son, Vyvyan Holland.

Again in Pont Street, no. 64 was the last home of the great actress Mrs Patrick Campbell from 1928-1940. It was indeed George Alexander who was responsible for her sensational debut at the St James's Theatre in 1893, when she appeared in Pinero's *The Second Mrs Tanqueray*. She had a famous relationship with George Bernard Shaw and one of her last major successes was as Eliza Doolittle in *Pygmalion* in 1914.

William Schwenk Gilbert (1836-1911), who with Sullivan ruled the light opera world at the turn of this century, lived in Pont Street for two years before his death trying to save a woman from drowning.

Dozens of London stage successes for over half a century owed their visual brilliance to the designs of Oliver Messel (1905-1978), who lived at 16 Yeomans Row from 1929 to 1946, and later at Pelham Place. He was the grandson of the Victorian artist, Linley Sambourne, and the uncle of Lord Snowdon.

Sir Herbert Beerbohm Tree (1852-1917), the great actor manager, took no. 2 Cheyne Walk for a short while in 1884 and was not at all pleased with it, complaining to the agent that vermin infested it. "My wife is frightened by beetles all evening and one cannot put anything down by way of work without animals crawling over it".

No theatrical partnership was more famous in its day than that of Lewis Casson and Sybil Thorndike. They had a house at 6 Carlyle Square from the 1920s, and a flat at Swan Court from 1962, both living to over ninety and much enjoying their role as grand dame and seigneur of the theatre.

The actress, Ellen Terry (1847-1928) lived at 215 Kings Road from 1904 to 1920, a house which happily survives between Glebe Place and Oakley Street and which has had many celebrated occupants over the years. Also in Kings Road a plaque on The Pheasantry records the occupancy of Serafina Astafieva, ballet dancer, who made her home in England in 1914 and two years later opened a Russian Dancing Academy here. Among her pupils were Anton Dolin, Alicia Markova, Harold Hasker and Margot Fonteyn. Diaghilev, who had many friends in Chelsea, used the studio here for rehearsals.

Two famous entertainers have enlivened Chelsea. The American, Ruth Draper (1884-1956), took a "darling house" at Swan Walk and lived at other times at Edith Grove and Carlyle Square; and Joyce Grenfell lived at 28 and then 21 St Leonard's Terrace, moving to nos 149 and then 114 Kings Road, followed by a flat at 34 Elm Park Gardens. Some of her early performances in revue were at the Royal Court.

160. H. Beerbohm Tree.

161. Ellen Terry.

Laurence Olivier had various homes in Chelsea, including 74 Cheyne Walk, Durham Cottage, Christchurch Street, as well as in St Leonard's Terrace and Mulberry Walk.

The film director Carol Reed (1906-1985) lived at 213 Kings Road. Another cinema connection was Judy Garland, who married her fifth husband at Chelsea Registry Office in 1969, only a few months before her death at her mews cottage, 4 Cadogan Lane.

No account of Chelsea's associations with theatre would be complete without a mention of Guy Boas, headmaster of the Sloane School for Boys for many years (1929-61), who put on Shakespearean productions by his pupils of such a professional standard that they became a highlight of the London year.

Guy Boas was appointed headmaster when he was only 32, having previously worked as Senior English Master at St Paul's Boys' School, and had already made a name for himself as a writer of books on Shakespearean acting. He became one of the first people to take the plays out of the classroom and on to a school stage, excelling in the training of boys to speak verse and using boys to play female parts in the traditional manner before this was generally accepted. A national critic wrote that Sloane School had "a special and recognised place in the theatre".

Guy Boas retired in 1961 and died in 1966 at the age of 69.

A FILM SET HOUSE

No. 52 Tite Street (More House) has starred in many films. It was built for the artist John Collier and his wife, Marion Huxley, in 1887. This preceded tragic events: Marion went mad and John eloped with her sister in the face of family disapproval. Before these happenings, however, he had made a strange house of five floors with labyrinthine passages and many unusual features which in later years attracted film and TV producers.

The house was bought by Adrian and Laura Troubridge in 1892, and it became a home for their grandson, Felix Hope-Nicholson, who tried to preserve it as a time capsule of a gracious past. Nevertheless, its many rooms were filled with lodgers selected by Mr Hope-Nicholson (described as a "host and genealogist") as being suitable to live in such a setting. They included at various times Clement Freud, Peter Quennell and Anthony Lambton.

Unfortunately, when Mr Hope-Nicholson died, attempts to acquire this unique feature of Chelsea failed, and it passed into private hands.

162. The Old Swan at Chelsea; by Walter Greaves 1858.

Pubs and Clubs

Comparing a James Hedderley photograph of the old Black Lion in Old Church Street with its Victorian replacement, Alfred Beaver commented in 1892 that "you can see at a glance what we are losing in this city of ours by gradual purposeless destruction of all that is delightful to the eye." He was spared the modern change of name to The Front Page! Beaver had also witnessed the destruction caused by the building of the Embankment and the gradual move of Chelsea from its riverside roots north and east to the Kings Road and to the Sloane Street developments. In this way a number of old pubs lost their traditional customers and some found that they were in areas that became increasingly slummy.

One of the oldest named pubs in Chelsea was the Swan, replaced by a brewery of the same name in 1780. It was to the original pub that Pepys travelled by road in April 1666 with his lady friends, "thinking to be merry", only to be warned on the way "that

163. The Black Lion at the corner of Paultons Street and Old Church Street, as it appeared in 1820, sketched by Alfred Beaver.

164. Playing 'Four Corners' at the Swan Inn in the eighteenth century; print published by Bowles.

the house was shut up with the sickness [plague]", and so they went back "with great fright" to Kensington. Here, too was the original finishing post for the Doggett's Coat and Badge race (see p.50). Smollett was fond of meeting his friends here in what must have been a congenial building with balconies overlooking the river, and skittles in its garden.

After the Swan's conversion to a brewhouse another inn, The Old Swan, was built on the west of the Physic Garden with a floating pier to allow steamboat passengers to disembark. This building was immortalised in the paintings of the Greaves brothers and Walter Burgess before it, and adjacent buildings were taken down to build the Embankment.

Not far away was the old Magpie and Stump, among the oldest of Chelsea's inns, Henry VIII having granted it a strip of land when he was lord of Chelsea manor. The 'Pye' as it was usually called, played an important part in local affairs for it was here that the sittings of the manor courts took place – the voluntary officers appointed at these were rewarded,

under the will of James Leverett, a retired gardener, with a dinner four times a year. In 1803 the inn was used by the conspirators, under Colonel Despard, plotting to kill George III and steal the Crown Jewels. The Pye survived the creation of the Embankment but was lost to a fire in 1886. Part of its site was used by the architect, C.R. Ashbee, to build a house for himself, and the skittle alley was converted into drawing offices. Sadly, this house was demolished in 1968, but houses next door, also by Ashbee, survive. A new Magpie and Stump is now at 442 Kings Road.

The Feathers in Chelsea is recorded in 1664. It was situated at what is now 49 Cheyne Walk. The Kings Head and Eight Bells on the corner of Cheyne Row was boasting in an 1871 photograph that it had been "established for over a century". Notices advertise Pale Ale at 4d a pint, Guinness and Bitter 2d. It was rebuilt in 1886 and still retains its old name.

On the corner of Lawrence Street at 51 Cheyne Walk, was the Thames Coffee House – far from

165. The King's Head and Eight Bells.

166. The Cricketers in Cheyne Walk; pencil and watercolour by J.T. Wilson, 1860s.

167. The Thames Coffee House in Cheyne Walk on the corner with Lawrence Street.

teetotal. The same row contained another inn, The Cricketers, which dated to at least the eighteenth century as the artist George Morland ("that unfortunate sot") paid for his drinks by painting an inn sign. This hung outside until 1824 when it was replaced by a crude copy, and the original was taken by the landlord to decorate the drinking booths he ran at race courses. When the lease of The Cricketers ran out the pub was replaced by "a huge ugly block of chambers" (Carlyle Mansions), in 1886.

The Greaves brothers and Burgess also immortalised the Adam and Eve, with its balconies overhanging the river near the old Ferry Wharf. Dating back to the seventeenth century, its walls were decorated with fowling pieces, relics of the days when duck shooting was a recreation for rich and poor alike and the Thames marshes alive with wild fowl.

In Old Church Street was the Black Lion, so missed by Beaver, on the corner of Paultons Street, probably built at the end of the seventeenth century, which became a popular venue for country outings, with its bowling green and tea gardens. Its near neighbour, the White Horse, an old posting house at the river end of the street, was visited by Charles Cheyne in 1669. The old timber-framed house burnt down in 1840 and was rebuilt.

The Cross Keys in Lawrence Street, whose name is said to commemorate a pottery mark of the nearby Chelsea China factory, is still there.

A newer pub near the river was the Pier Hotel on the corner of Oakley Street, by Albert Bridge, when steamboat travel was at the height of its popularity. This was demolished in 1968, along with another Chelsea landmark, the Blue Cockatoo, to build Pier House flats. Happily, the artist, Cecil Lawson, portrayed The Bell, on the corner of Danvers Street

168. *The Cross Keys in Lawrence Street.*

169. *The Royal Hospital pub; pencil and watercolour by John Crowther, 1900.*

170. The early World's End pub.

171. The World's End early this century.

172. Advertisement for the revived Chelsea Arts Ball at the Royal Albert Hall in 1984.

and Cheyne Walk in 1874 before it was demolished. The Aquatic Tavern was next door to the small house by the river to which Turner retreated (see p.99) and was probably the last hostelry before the wharves and the creek which separated Chelsea from Fulham.

Compared to the large number of pubs near the river, those of 'inland' Chelsea were few. The World's End was one of the best known, its name indicating that the next place of refreshment going out of London was some distance away. There have been three inns on this site, the first a wooden building, possibly that referred to by Mrs Frail in Congreve's *Love for Love*. By the 1870s the World's End was a solid Victorian gin palace. Travellers had another chance of refreshment nearby at the Man in the Moon, and at the Globe in Milmans Street (now the Water Rat). What used to be the Six Bells in Kings Road has its origin as an eighteenth-century inn, which became a favourite place for Whistler and others. In 1900 it was rebuilt in Tudor style.

THE CHELSEA ARTS CLUB

In 1891 a group of artists, led by the sculptor Thomas Lee, decided to form a club to meet at the premises of another of their number, the Scots painter, James Christie, at 181 Kings Road. Founder members included Whistler, Sickert, Clausen and Steer. It was a great success, despite its strict rule that only those with a genuine connection with the visual arts were eligible for membership, and its purposes were social and not promotional.

In 1902 the Club moved to 143 Old Church Street, one of the most attractive remnants of Chelsea village, with a secluded garden now enhanced by a fountain by Henry Pool. Members have included Henry Tonks, the 'terrible Tonks' who struck fear into the hearts of his Slade students, who lived in The Vale, and John Singer Sargent. The Club insti-

tuted an annual fancy dress party, which soon outgrew the premises and moved on to Chelsea Town Hall and the Royal Albert Hall, where it took place from 1908 to the 1950s.

173. The Chenil Galleries in Kings Road.

THE CHENIL GALLERIES
In the 1890s, another meeting place of artists was Charles Chenil's artists' materials' shop at 183 Kings Road, between the Town Hall and the Six Bells. In 1905 a permanent gallery was opened here. The driving force of this venture was John Knewstub, a north countryman whose father had worked for Rossetti, and whose sisters were married to William Orpen and William Rothenstein. For ten years the gallery was the hub of Chelsea artistic life. One room there housed a collection of the group of which Orpen was a leading member, and the other held more transitory exhibitions. Other names associated with the Chenil at this period were Eric Gill, Mark Gertler and Roger Fry. From 1910 Augustus John had a studio here.

Of the first solo exhibition here of David Bomberg in 1914 (one canvass was too large to get through the door and was exhibited outside), the *Daily Chronicle* opined that those who visited such shows were not the public but "youthful, eager artists with strange hats and strong opinions".

After the 1st World War Knewstub resurrected his enterprise to extend it to include a concert hall, workshops and a library, taking over the former premises of the Chelsea Arts Club. In its heyday John

Drinkwater gave poetry readings, Barbirolli conducted concerts and the Sitwells presented *Facade*, with Diaghilev in the audience. However, the heyday was a short one and the galleries were in the hands of the receivers within two years. During the last war the premises were used for Civil Defence and shortly after sold to the council and used for art exhibitions, X-ray sessions and charity events. In 1977 they were sold to a private owner as an antique centre.

THE PHEASANTRY
From its establishment as a club in 1932 to its sad demise in 1966, The Pheasantry in Kings Road epitomised the old spirit of Chelsea. René de Meo, who took over the premises when the old interior decorating business left, created something unique, according to its historian, Nesta Macdonald, who fought so devotedly to save it in the 1970s. "He not only created a restaurant but a club and he and his successors kept it going for nearly thirty-five years." In its atmosphere of rather gloomy intimacy, the famous and would-be famous rubbed shoulders. In the earliest days it was Augustus John who ruled, and later it was Annigoni. Other habitués included Dylan Thomas and his wife Caitlin, the ballerina Beryl Grey, the singer Gigli and Peter Ustinov.

Subscriptions cost 10s 6d for artists, fifteen shillings for ladies and a guinea for gentlemen; the food included shish kebab served on a flaming sword for 7s 6d.

But it all ended too soon. In 1958, René de Meo had a heart attack and the club was carried on by his partner, Mario Cazzini, until his death in 1966. Before long the Pheasantry was a sorry sight, though it was a Grade II listed building. Amid the sixties glitter of the Kings Road it stood like an old ghost, surrounded by corrugated iron, defaced by fly-posters and insulted by graffiti. Buyers, sellers and schemes came and went, many seen off by Nesta Macdonald, but it was saved from the bulldozers. It is now a restaurant.

THE LONDON SKETCH CLUB
The London Sketch Club has been situated in Dilke Street for about forty years. It has its roots in the Langham Sketch Club founded in 1838, whose members were drawn from those working for *Punch* and *The Yellow Book* and other periodicals, which met first at a gallery in Bond Street.

174. *A derelict Pheasantry in the Kings Road; drawn by Timothy Whidborne in 1977.*

175. *Interior of The Pheasantry in its heyday.*

176. *James Pilton's Manufactory, from The Gentleman's Magazine in 1809.*

Works and Workers

Chelsea has some manufacturing history, including an armaments factory founded by two brothers named Engilbert. They "invented certain engines of war" and set up business somewhere in Chelsea where they took premises in 1564 to "make Her Majesty's engines". These were described as being able to fire missiles from a mile distance "as well by night as by day", which would "burst and blow up houses in such terrible sort that it would not be possible for anyone to live there the terror would be so great."

In 1761, when the vestry decided that the church bells needed recasting, the job was given to Thomas Janaway, whose foundry was situated in World's End Passage, where he also made heavy siege guns.

The best known Chelsea manufacturer however must be Thomas Crapper, who set up his 'Sanitary engineering' business in Marlborough Road in 1861 with three shops, a yard and a brass foundry, where he could cast valves and other metal work for his water closets.

Flush toilets had been installed in some larger houses for over half a century, but their mechanics were not always reliable. Crapper, however, promised a 'Certain flush with every pull'.

Crapper was only eleven when he walked to London from Doncaster to seek his fortune. He apprenticed himself to a plumber in Sydney Street, being paid four shillings a week, and he was twenty-four when he set up his own business. He was eventually to hold the royal warrant as plumber to Victoria, Edward VII and George V. It was Crapper who introduced floral lavatory bowls, mahogany seats and pedestals approached up steps as though to a throne: Lily Langtry had a velvet upholstered version. In 1907 the firm moved to 120 Kings Road, where it remained until 1966.

Numerous craftsmen worked in the roads to the west of Sloane Street. These included John Birnie Philip, who took the kitchen of Henry Holland's old house to produce the 99 figures he made for the Albert Memorial.

William Willett (1856-1915), famous for inventing 'daylight saving', was by trade a builder and architect. His business was in Sloane Square (marked by a plaque).

An advertisement in the *Gentleman's Magazine* in 1809 announced the availability of ornamental works for country residences at the Manor House in Manor Street. This was James Pilton's Manufactory, which also had showrooms in Piccadilly. His "invisible wire fences" were intended to house collections of ornamental birds. There were several linoleum factories, two of them in the Kings Road. The Wilkinson Sword Company made bicycles when they had their works in Kings Road on the corner of Sydney Street.

Horse traffic demanded the presence of forges and one of the last of these to survive in Chelsea was Margries, first established in Flood Street in 1864, moving to Dovehouse Street in 1888, and finally to a site near the Pier Hotel. The business had sensibly switched by then to ornamental iron work and the making of armatures for sculptors.

Fun and Games

THE PENSIONERS

They called it Chelsea Football Club, though it was in Fulham. Its founders, who hoped that it would prove to be "one of the most important and successful teams in London", were H.A. ('Gus') and J.T. (Joseph) Mears, constructional engineers, whose firm built the Fulham river embankment. They had dreamed of establishing a football club since the mid 1890s, but it was not until 1904 that they leased the site of the old London Athletic Club beside the West London railway line, between Lillie Road and Fulham Road. At that time the Mears brothers had plans for a stadium accommodating 100,000, and they promised to obtain first-class players.

Chelsea played in their first League match against West Bromwich Albion, and by the 1906/7 season, when a crowd of 60,000 watched them play Manchester United, they had reached the First Division. Their first big success, however, was nearly fifty years later when they were League champions, and in 1970 they won the FA Cup, followed by the European Cup

Winners Cup in the next two years. They have, however, almost always been in the news – of late often because of the chronic uncertainty over the future of the Stamford Bridge ground.

This has now been resolved and there is also some hope that the traffic congestion on match days can be eased by the opening of a station on any new railway line. 'Chelsea Village', a scheme drawn up by KSS Architects, will surround the pitch with a complex of stands, restaurants and cafés, as well as a sports centre, a 160-bedroom hotel, a large car park and some residential development.

PRINCES SPORTS CLUB

This club was established in the 1870s on part of the grounds of Henry Holland's old house (see p.117). It had no royal connections, being named for its owners, George and James Prince. It began as a cricket club – *Wisden* recommended its pitch as "one of the truest in England" and the MCC played there for a while before moving to their own ground at Lords. Tennis and badminton, and later skating on artificial ice, were added to the facilities in the following years, though membership remained exclusive. Women were only accepted if they had been

177. The half-mile race at the Civil Service Sports event at Stamford Bridge in the 1920s.

178. The Chelsea football team in 1905.

179. Advertisement for the South Kensington and Chelsea Cycle Supply and Instruction Co., from a street directory.

THE . . . . .

South Kensington and Chelsea Cycle Supply and Instruction Co.

LIMITED,

CHELSEA CLUB HALL,

155, FULHAM ROAD.

(Near South Kensington Station.)

Cycling Lessons

Daily, by Experienced Instructors.

Bicycles on Sale or Hire.

180. At the Glaciarium in Kings Road; from the Illustrated London News 13 May 1876.

presented at Court; charges were high and the admission limited so that a "skating wife would not be allowed to bring in her husband or daughter".

The lease of the premises was, however, short and in 1885 the Princes Club moved to West Kensington, where it did borrow from the royals and renamed itself the Queen's Club. The Princes Club land was then used to build Lennox Gardens and Cadogan Square.

ENERGETIC PEOPLE

Chelsea had two skating rinks apart from that at the Princes Club. One at Royal Avenue, opened in 1875, offered a rink of 3000 square yards covered with Green's Patent Ice, and in 1876 the Glaciarium, in Milmans Street, was run by John Gamgee who claimed to use "real ice" in a tent-like arena made "artificially cold".

Cycling featured prominently. At 151 Fulham Road the South Kensington and Chelsea Supply and Instruction Company not only sold bikes but taught people how to ride them, and at the Cycledom Riding School in Kings Road, cyclists were initiated into the arts of starting, balancing, riding, mounting and dismounting. *The Wheelwoman* noted in 1896 that the "prettily decorated hall was bright and animated with the rapidly moving figures of teachers and taught. Some of the best known cyclists in society have graduated from this Cycledom with graceful, courageous riding."

The medical profession gave its blessing to cycling as a healthy pursuit even then, with two local doctors, Dr Redmond and Dr Gunton, forming the Carlyle Cycling Club, first at Gertrude Street, then at the Six Bells in 1900. The first members were mainly constables from Chelsea Police Station but later women members were allowed.

Blitz Diary

During the London Blitz Josephine May Oakman, made a diary of events which, happily, was deposited in the Chelsea borough archives. She had lived in Chelsea for 45 years and worked in the Food Office during the war and as a part time Air Raid Warden. Her experiences – transcribed by her nephew Alan Wharam – recall the day-to-day happenings of those times and not just the dramatic days and nights.

Among the first incidents recorded is that on 8 September 1940, when bombs fell on Cadogan Square and Pont Street. The next afternoon it was the turn of Beaufort Street. "Three awful bursts, God help them, one at Cadogan House shelter. I did some stretcher work – counted the poor bodies, 57 of them including our own warden". Less than four hours later she was back on duty at Bramerton Street. "The Rev. Arrowsmith came and worked on the heap of wreckage (seven people were trapped) until his hands were bleeding." The following night horses died in burning stables at Petyt Place.

Friday 13 September lived up to its superstitious reputation when four people were drowned by a burst water main at Chelsea Manor Buildings. Even worse was to come the next day when just after six on a lovely evening, a bomb fell on the Church of Our Most Holy Redeemer in Cheyne Row, where nearly a hundred people were sheltering. "I think my heart broke that night", she wrote. When she eventually returned to her own home she found that it too had been destroyed.

On 5 October she noted that Chelsea had had four weeks of raids, and on 15 October there were thirty incidents, including one at St Stephen's Hospital, which suffered badly from enemy action, the damage to two ward blocks being so severe that they had to be demolished, and there was a high toll of death and injury among both staff and patients.

One night Jo Oakman spent at Paultons Square trench shelter. "The Rev. Newsome is always there and sleeps among the hundreds who have taken shelter."

On 7 November a bomb fell on Shawfield Street, killing twelve and a few days later another fell on Sloane Square station while two trains were standing at the platforms. "The whole station – just rebuilt – collapsed on the line – nothing left but the iron girders." The roll of dead was horrendous.

The largest of her diaries covers the period of the flying bombs. On 23 February 1944 four bombs fell at World's End, one of which hit the Guinness Trust flats; this was the worst single incident in Chelsea, she says, "with 86 people killed and over a hundred injured."

181. A temporary bridge erected on the Thames at Chelsea; illustration by Jo Oakman.

"Mystery explosions" in September 1944 preceded by a rumble like thunder, heralded the arrival of the first V2 rockets known as 'flying gas mains' as at first security decreed that they should be described as gas main explosions.

At the end of the war Jo Oakman was allowed to keep her tin hat and gas mask, considering that the former might make a "nice geranium pot".

The Royal Hospital had been hit by one of the relatively few bombs which fell in London during the First World War. The incident occurred in February 1918, when a 500lb bomb destroyed the north-east wing of Light Horse Court – the target of another bomb in 1945. During the Second World War there was a near miss on the Infirmary in October 1940. This was followed ten days later by bombs which hit the main staircase and east wing. On 16 April 1941, the same night that saw the destruction of the Old Church, a land mine destroyed the east wing of the Infirmary, killing the Ward Master, eight pensioners and four nurses, with 37 other casualties.

In January 1945 a V2 rocket blew up the north-east wing of the Light Horse Court, with four fatalities and 19 injured – a final blow to the ancient structure and its ageing inhabitants.

A TRAITOR IN OUR MIDST

Bramerton Street was one of the several Chelsea homes of William Joyce (Lord Haw-Haw), who became a propagandist for the Nazis. He also lived in Flood Street and Jubilee Place.

Born in New York in 1906, the main plank of Joyce's defence on a charge of treason in 1945 was that he was an American citizen. Indeed he was, for he had never renounced his American citizenship. But he did travel on a British passport which, though illegal, was deemed to have required his allegiance to the Crown, and this was enough to ensure that he was hanged at Wandsworth prison in 1946.

Looking After Chelsea

A MATTER OF BOUNDARIES

Chelsea used to be larger. A bequest dating back to the time of Edward the Confessor granted the manor of Chelsea 130 acres of woodland on the northern edge of Kensington. This area, known as the Chelsea Outlands, remained a part of the parish of Chelsea until the end of the nineteenth century, and was the site of Kensal New Town. When the London boroughs were reorganised in 1899, this area was given to Kensington, which was none too pleased with the gift since by then the district was poverty-stricken and a burden on the municipal rates.

Relationships with Kensington were further tested when the London boroughs were once again reorganised in 1965. The motto *Quam bonum in unum habitare* ('What a good thing it is to dwell together in unity') was a pious hope when Chelsea was united with Kensington in the wholescale changes of that year. Chelsea felt relegated to second place in the new borough, emphasised in the name of the Royal Borough of Kensington and Chelsea. Soon, Chelsea Town Hall became merely a municipal outbuilding, rather than a centre of local government. Even the Chelsea library, already restricted in Space, was moved from its original building to an even smaller area in the old Town Hall.

In 1996 further changes to borough boundaries have come into force. Some streets on its western border have moved into Hammersmith and Fulham, including flats and studios between Wandon Road and the railway.

At least the Parliamentary constituency has remained the same in name – Kensington & Chelsea – even if the boundaries have been changed. It has been a safe Conservative seat, held by Nicholas Scott since 1974.

REPELLING INVADERS

The new borough and the inevitably less intimate relationships with the local authority, as far as Chelsea residents are concerned, have given yet more impetus to the work of the Chelsea Society.

Chelsea has been under threat of redevelopment since the construction of the Embankment, which ensured, for better or for worse, that Chelsea's picturesque riverside disappeared for ever. At that time, protests against the changes were of an individual nature, but since 1927 the redoubtable Chelsea Society has existed to assess and, if necessary, co-ordinate opposition to schemes to develop parts of Chelsea. The Society was founded by the Chelsea historian, Reginald Blunt, and subsequent defenders of Chelsea have included well-known artists and writers as well as the affluent who have increasingly moved westward from Mayfair and Belgravia.

The Society is particularly involved at the moment in the proposal to make the whole of the Kings Road a Conservation Area so that it may be considered as a single entity; it is particularly concerned about the future of the King's College site, which it has fought for many years to preserve for educational use, and the opening of huge new restaurants in what is still primarily a residential area. The Society also gave evidence at the inquiry into a planning application to construct a 20-storey block of flats on the site of Battersea Flour Mills, across the river from Cheyne Walk.

Also founded in 1927 was the Chelsea Gardens Guild, which encourages amateur gardeners with advice and lectures, even if the result is only a window box.

The greatest threat to Chelsea, other than the constant commercial exploitation, has been yet another road. In the 1970s the proposed West Cross route seemed likely to thrust a motorway through the western boundary between Chelsea and Fulham but without, however, any new bridge over the river to take the traffic it would encourage. Eventually economic circumstances, rather than anything else, caused the abandonment of the proposal, and the subsequent construction of Chelsea Harbour makes it certain that whatever solution is proposed to ease traffic congestion, it will not now be the West Cross route.

Property values have proved the undoing of the studio accommodation on which so many artists, and especially sculptors, relied. Nowhere has the loss of such spaces been so prevalent as in Chelsea, where hundreds of studios have become residences rather than work places.

With all this Chelsea retains an undeniable charm and character worthy of its role as a backdrop to many dramas in English history. There are still corners which keep much the same appearance as they did a century or more ago, although the feel of the place is one of looking forward. Those who live and work there include many of today's history makers in the worlds of politics, science and the arts, and although the village of palaces has faded, its spirit survives.

INDEX

Illustrations or captions are indicated by an asterisk